Hidd   ....s.

The First Century Jewish Way of
Understanding the Scriptures

Hidden Treasures:

The First Century Jewish Way of Understanding the Scriptures

Joseph Shulam

Netivyah Bible Instruction Ministry
Jerusalem, Israel
2008

Netivyah Bible Instruction Ministry

NETIVYAH
P.O. Box 8043
Jerusalem, 91080
ISRAEL

NETIVYAH U.S.A.
P.O. Box 1387
Mt. Juliet, TN 37121
U.S.A.

netivyah@netivyah.org.il
www.netivyah.org

ISBN (978-0-9818730-0-8)

Hidden Treasures: The First Century Jewish Way
of Understanding the Scriptures, by Joseph Shulam

Editors: Elizabeth Wakefield, Rittie Katz

Printed in Israel

I dedicate this book to Marcia my wife of forty years.
Marcia is the woman by my side and my inspiration!

Joseph Shulam

Contents

Introduction

Netivyah Bible Instruction Ministry is located in the center of Jerusalem. A cursory look at the city today may give one the correct impression of a thriving cosmopolitan metropolis, complete with red tile roofed houses and the requisite cell phone for each person. To look at Jerusalem only today, however, would be to miss the layer upon layer of civilization, conflict, hope, dreams, loss, aspirations, and prayers that have been part of the life of the City from the beginning. Jerusalem was captured by King David and made the political and religious capital of the Jewish people. Jerusalem is the home of the First Temple built by King Solomon, as well as the Second Temple. Jerusalem has been destroyed by civil wars, conquered by the Babylonians, Romans, Crusaders, Muslims, British, and many others. It was divided in 1948 at the inception of the modern State of Israel and re-united in 1967. Jerusalem is now a vibrant and pulsating metropolis. It is the home of three major world religions and the stage on which the Lord Yeshua has changed and will continue to change history. No city the whole world over is more beautiful or more steeped in controversy than Jerusalem. To ignore the historical, religious, cultural, and prophetic implications of Jerusalem is to miss the heart and the essence of the history of salvation.

Similarly, to read the Bible and content ourselves with only the traditional Christian theological understanding is to perhaps miss the root and essence of God's revelation in the Scriptures themselves. The traditional way that Christians have understood the Bible has brought division and sectarianism into the world. In this book, Joseph Shulam gives the reader tools with which to dig deeply into the First Century background of the Scriptures. This book will enable the reader to piece together the hidden layers and meaning contained within the sacred texts.

This book is divided into two parts. The first section gives a basic introduction to the subjects of hermeneutics and Biblical interpretation, and explains how Jewish interpretation helps us better understand the New Testament text. The book has chapters explaining the exegetical principles of Rabbi Hillel, a famous First Century Rabbi who was the president of the Sanhedrin. It also explains the concept of *midrash* and the four Rabbinic levels of interpretation. This volume will provide the reader with useful tools for personal study, academic endeavors, and Biblical exegesis. The reader will find many examples of how the New Testament authors used traditional Jewish exegetical methods to construct their arguments from the Torah, the Prophets, and the Psalms.

The second section contains articles on important contemporary issues for disciples of Yeshua. Some of these topics include how we can restore a uniquely Messianic hermeneutic. Many problems that beset Christian theologians can find their solution by seeing the New Testament as a Jewish book. The problem of balancing observance of God's commandments with the grace we have in Yeshua the Messiah can be resolved by reading Paul's letters in the context of his Jewish Rabbinic background. Finally, there is a chapter on the importance of continuous education in Jewish life.

The title of this book comes from **Isaiah 45:3**, which says, "*And I will give you the treasures of darkness and hidden riches of secret places that you may know that I, the Lord, who calls you by name, am the God of Israel.*"

May you be enriched and strengthened as you embark on this journey of discovery.   -The Editors

The Writer's Forward

The Bible is a collection of ancient literature. It was written over a period of a thousand years and by many different writers under many different circumstances. Naturally, if such an ancient document fell into the hands of any modern reader, he would find it difficult to decipher, read, or understand. In order to be able to understand the Bible, the science of hermeneutics developed both in Christianity and in Judaism. The New Testament was written almost exclusively by Jews in a Jewish Historical context, and it reflects the ideas and the concepts of the Jewish people during the First Century after Yeshua.

This book, although small in volume, is a collection of articles which I hope will enable you to take a significant step in furthering your understanding of the Bible and give you tools to better understand the Word of God as it was intended to be understood by the writers themselves.

In a sense, these eight chapters are a synthesis of teachings and lectures given in lay circles over the last few years. Rabbi Paul states in **2 Timothy 2:15**, we must rightly divide the word of truth. What does this mean? If I put Paul's statement to "rightly divide the Word of Truth" into simple terms, it means to read the Word of God without making a salad out of it. It means that we ought to discern the difference between poetry and narratives in the Bible. It means that we ought to put things into their historical setting the best we can before we produce doctrines that divide the body of believers based on uneducated opinions. It means that we ought to divide between things that are eternal and things that are ad-hoc and only for a specific occasion.

The Apostle Paul states in the New Testament: *"What advantage, then, is there in being a Jew, or what value is there in circumcision? Much in every way! First of all, they have been entrusted with the very words of God."* **(Romans 3:1-2)** I believe that appreciating the way in which Jewish people have related to and interpreted the Bible, as well as the cultural and historical context in which it was written, will enhance your awareness of the methods that were used by the writers of the Scriptures.

Many of us have literally staked our lives on what is written in the Bible. Especially in Israel, we have been marginalized, rejected, persecuted, and maligned. It is, therefore, incumbent upon us to truly understand the precepts within the Scriptures, and in the event that we are asked, to give an answer for the hope that is within us.

Rabbi Paul studied under the great teacher Gamliel who was the grandson of Hillel. The first principles of hermeneutics (Biblical interpretation) in Judaism contained in this book were codified by Rabbi Hillel. The rules of interpretation that were used by the New Testament writers are those same rules that were used by all the Jewish interpreters of the Torah and the Prophets. For this very reason, we ought to make a special effort to understand these rules and use them in order to better comprehend God's Word.

The attitude of the Rabbis toward the Torah (Law of Moses) and the commandments seems to always be in question by Christians and Jews. As a part of this "forward," I would like to introduce to you an interesting *midrash* that will bring you into the world of the Rabbis and demonstrate the spirit of the Torah and a certain unique way of dealing with the Scriptures.

The Lord was wondering how He could know which of His servants serve Him out of fear and which of them serve Him out of love. He devised a method that would discover this knowledge. He built a room four by four, a four-square room with only one small peep hole of four by four spans. The Lord put all His servants into this room. Those servants who served Him out of fear stood in that "four by four" room and said: "If the Lord had wanted us to break out of this room He would not have built it and put us into it." The servants who loved the Lord said, "We want to break out of this room and join the Lord in the outside in the wide open spaces." However the little peep hole was too small, and they had to make themselves suffer and lose much weight to be able to fit through the small peep hole in the door and join the Lord in the wide open spaces. They loved the Lord so much that they could not stay closed in the "four by four" room even knowing that the Lord had built it and placed them there.[I] They wanted to "break out" by force and violence from the "four by four" room and join the Lord who was sitting on His throne in the wide open spaces.

This *midrash* is very interesting in many ways. The first important truth from this *midrash* is that it is based on the text of **Micah 2:12-13**, *"I will surely assemble all of you, O Jacob, I will surely gather the remnant of Israel; I will put them together like sheep of the fold, like a flock in the midst of their pasture. They shall make a loud noise because of so many people. The one who breaks open will come up before them; they will break out. Pass through the gate, and go out by it; their king will pass before them, with the LORD at their head."* The use of the word, "breaker" or "poretz" in Hebrew, which also means "violent man," brings us to Yeshua's words

I   Tana Debi Eliyahu, Ish-Shalom Edition, p. 82.

in the Gospel of **Matthew 11:12**, *"And from the days of John the Baptist until now the kingdom of heaven suffers violence, and the violent take it by force."* The Prophet Micah says that God will put Israel in the "sheep fold." Then the "one that breaks open" will "go out," and *"their King will pass before them, with the LORD at their head."* The whole story from the *midrash* is here in the words of Micah the prophet. Yeshua captures the story by describing the entrance into the Kingdom of God as a forceful, violent act of breaking out and entering the realm where the King is, outside of the fold. Here, therefore, we have a Rabbinic use of the text of Micah in the framework of a "parable" that demonstrates the words of the Prophet in relationship to the King and the Lord who walks out before the whole multitude.

This text from the *Tana Debi Eliyahu Midrash* is a good demonstration of two major themes: 1) God is not a legalist. Those who love Him are those who want to be with Him in the wide open spaces much more than they want to be under the legal protection of the bounds of Torah Commandments. 2) It is of greater importance to love God than to be enclosed by the *halacha* (the legal system) of the Torah.

The study of "how to understand and interpret the Scriptures" is a challenge for every serious student of the Scriptures. This book is written in order to help the reader understand and dive into the world of Yeshua and into the First Century methods of understanding the Oracles of God.

May God strengthen your faith, your understanding, your wisdom, and your courage as you endeavor to know the Lord in a deeper way and to serve Him in spirit and in truth.

-Joseph Shulam

Part One:

Jewish Interpretive Methods
for Sacred Texts

Chapter 1:

An Introduction to Hermeneutics

The subject of hermeneutics is very important because it determines how we understand the Bible. It could be classified both as an art and a science, but either way it refers to the methods we use to study and understand a text. According to the *Anchor Bible Dictionary*, hermeneutics is "the art of understanding... It can refer to the conditions which make understanding possible and even to the process of understanding as a whole."[II]

Every time we read the words someone else wrote, we have to "translate" them within our own brains so we can understand their meaning. Any sort of "translation" also naturally demands interpretation, so good hermeneutical methods should enable us to grasp a meaning as close as possible to the author's original intent. This process becomes much more difficult with the Bible because we must try to discern the intents of both the Divine and human authors in the original context and apply the text to our lives in our own modern context, as well.

The way a person understands the Bible is generally greatly influenced by their cultural and religious background. The way a Jew understands the Bible is not necessarily the same way a Christian would interpret the same text. The time period in which people live has an impact upon their interpretation of God's Word. Even with all the difficulties involved in trying to accurately interpret parts of the Bible

II   Lategan, Bernard C. "Hermeneutics." *ABD*. Vol. 3. London: Doubleday, 1992, p. 155.

that are sometimes difficult to understand, we should be very thankful that we have such easy access to the written Word of God so that guidance and help from Him is "at the tips of our fingers" on a daily basis.

Back in Old Testament times, someone who wanted to know the will of God had to do much more than simply open a Bible. The people did not have Torah scrolls in their houses, so they had to go to their prophets and priests who were the means of communication between God and the people and the people and God. They did not have a text. Either the prophet would give them God's answer, or the priest would use the instruments of the Urim and Thurim to tell them "yes" or "no." There was also a way to use the priest's breastplate with the twelve precious stones to get God's response to their questions.

I live on a hill outside Jerusalem, and right below my house a natural spring emerges from the earth. This is the exact same spring from the Ramah of Biblical times where Saul and his servants went to look for their lost donkeys in **1 Samuel 9**. Verse 6 of that chapter says that after fruitlessly searching for some time, Saul's servant said to him, *"Behold, there is a man of God in this city, and he is a man who is held in honor; all that he says comes true. So now let us go there. Perhaps he can tell us the way we should go."* This is an example of people going to the prophet when they needed supernatural help with their problems. The Tanach never says anywhere, "Anyone who wants to know the will of God should read the text of the Bible."

The disciples of Yeshua today are influenced by a very Protestant world view. Martin Luther and the Protestant Reformation have changed the way that we look at communication with God. Like the Pharisees of the First

Century BCE and CE (=AD), the Protestant Reformation actually concentrated on communication with God through the text of the word of God. This is not generally true for people from the Catholic persuasion. The main communication in the historical churches (Catholic and Orthodox) of the people with God is through the agency of the Priest. This position is changing and being modified all the time, even in the Catholic Church. The Vatican II Council reversed the previous Church dictum that recommended that people not read the Bible. In many parts of the Catholic world, however, many people still rely on their priests to tell them the will of God. In fact, reading the Word of God is not considered a way to discern the will of God for the general public.

It may come as a surprise to many students of the Bible that the first group of people who began studying the text of the Scriptures in order to know God's will were the Pharisees in Jerusalem. They created a revolution in understanding the will of God because they said that the Bible was for everyone and not just for prophets and priests. The concept of an individual being able to read the Bible and find out the will of God by analyzing the text with his mind, with logic, and with an emphasis on grammar and language, was a great and fantastic revolution that the Pharisees created.

Today almost everyone has Bibles, and most languages even have several different translations as well. In Biblical times, however, the people did not have the books of the Bible, not even the Torah, in their possession. The Torah was inside the Temple, and only the priests studied it. The average farmer in the Galilee had never seen a Torah scroll. Only the priests and the members of the school of the prophets could study the Word of God, and most of them probably did not even have the entire text of the Bible at their disposal. It was only after the Maccabean revolt against the Greeks and the first Chanukah in the Second Century BCE that the Pharisees had the revolutionary idea that "the Bible is for everyone!"

One might ask why personal interpretation and study of the Bible and the forming of *midrash* became popular exactly at that time and not beforehand. Professor Michael Fishbane of the University of Chicago explains it this way: "The closure of the scriptural canon (by the beginning of the common era) changes matters fundamentally. It is a transformative event, for with this closure there can be no new additions or supplementations to the biblical text from without... The result is that the extended (but bounded) speech of Scripture is reconceived of as the multiform expressions of divine revelation- beginning with the individual letters of its words, and including all the phrases and sentences of Scripture. These all become the constituents of possibility in the opening of Scripture *from within*."[III]

Since the Third Century BCE, there has been a tradition of Biblical interpretation. Everyone has a tradition for how to understand the Bible, whether he learned it formally from a teacher or not. This rich tradition of interpretation can be very helpful when encountering a difficult text, but it can also close a person's mind to the possibility of an alternative interpretation that he simply has never heard before.

The Method of PARDES

No matter what a text's origins are, every single one of them has many options for interpretation. For example, when most people read a newspaper, they understand its simple meaning. Whatever it says is usually what it means, and most people do

---

III   Fishbane, Michael. "*Midrash* and the Meaning of Scripture." *The Interpretation of the Bible: The International Symposium in Slovenia.* Ed. Joe Krasovec. Sheffield: Sheffield Academic Press, 1998, p. 552.

not try to read between the lines in a simple news story. On the other hand, anyone who knows the writers personally or who has personally experienced the events behind the written story understands what is not said in the text. He can understand what is only hinted at in the text. Every text has the plain meaning and the hidden and hinted meaning, which at times can only be discerned (from) between the lines. Lawyers are experts in this area. They see the hidden meaning that the average person who does not understand the legal texts cannot grasp at first reading. Ordinary people have to concentrate and read the texts many times in order to understand the nuances. Every text has the plain, obvious meaning as well as the hidden and hinted meaning.

Some texts even have secret messages imbedded in them. One of my cousins used to be a lawyer in Bulgaria. Even though I had not had contact with him for four or five years, one night I got a telephone call from Bulgaria. He said, "I have a birthday coming up soon, and I would like for you to buy me a birthday gift. You can buy me a plastic airplane or a plastic boat." I am sure that the KGB was listening to him, and he knew that the KGB was listening to him, too! I immediately understood what he meant, so I asked him if he wanted to celebrate his birthday in an Italian or a Greek restaurant. Since I knew him and knew when his real birthday was, I understood what he meant in this conversation. He was telling me that he wanted to get out of Bulgaria, so I asked him if he wanted to run away through Italy or Greece. The entire conversation was encoded though, so anyone who did not know him personally could not have understood what we were talking about.

Thus far we have examined three methods of interpretation. One method studies the Biblical text using the plain, grammatical meaning of the words, and this method is called "*p'shat*," which means "simple or literary." Second, there is the meaning at which the texts hint, although it is not stated obviously. This indirect method is called "*remez*" in Hebrew. Then thirdly, there can also be a secret meaning that only the initiated can understand. Hebrew refers to this as "*sod*," which means "secret." There is also a fourth kind of understanding called "*drash*," which means "association." This level of understanding is not strictly what is written, nor the secret meaning, nor the hinted at meaning. It is rather what the text reminds a person of when it is read. The *drash* method examines not only the main text that is being studied or expounded but also any other sacred texts that are associated with the main text. When one associates these texts together, he can learn something that he had not understood previously. *Drash* is the most difficult method to conceptualize because it requires understanding the connection between the two texts.

Here is one illustration of this fourth method. When Yeshua was born in Bethlehem, and Herod heard about it, he wanted to eliminate the possibility of any other king reigning in Israel. Therefore, he ordered all the babies up to the age of two to be killed in Bethlehem. An angel came to Joseph in a dream and warned him about this danger, so Joseph and Miriam took Yeshua and fled to Egypt. A few years later an angel told them that Herod had died and that they should return to Israel. When Matthew describes this event, he says that it happened to fulfill a text in Hosea which says, "*Out of Egypt I have called my son.*" Many interpreters have puzzled over this problem for a long time because the original text in **Hosea 11** has absolutely nothing to do with Yeshua. In fact, the text has a very negative context when it is used in Hosea. What happened here was that Yeshua was called out of Egypt, and the children of Israel who are also referred to as "sons of God" were called out of Egypt as well. Matthew associated one event with the words of the other text referring to a previous event and made a *midrash* using associative logic. Relating "*coming out of Egypt*" with the text in Hosea that has the same words is useful to connect the two historical events and their parallels.

One common psychological test is to give patients words and ask them what they associate with these words. They test the associations people have with different emotions. Everyone uses associative logic because different triggers cause different associations in each individual mind. The same thing is true of texts. Each Biblical text contains certain elements that trigger associations in us. For example, when I read about Elijah the prophet eating locust, I immediately remember all the wonderful times I had when I ate locust. It is a tasty kosher food, and it reminds me of certain events in my life. When I read about the circumcision of John the Baptist, I remember when I circumcised my son. There are not only experiential associations, however; there are also textual associations in which a word in one text reminds the reader of another text.

Therefore, there are four basic Jewish hermeneutical levels, which are together called "*pardes*" "orchard." The "P" is for "*pshat*," the "R" is for "*remez*," "D" is for "*drash*," and "S" is for "*sod*." This term is the basis of Jewish hermeneutics and every text, whether it appears in the newspaper, a novel, or the Bible, consists of these elements.

Association and Allegorical Interpretation

Christian seminaries usually teach only the normal Protestant hermeneutic, which concentrates exclusively on the most literal and simple understanding of the text. Sometimes they also utilize a Greek method, in which they spiritualize the text and make an allegory out of it. In so doing, the text loses its historical significance and meaning and becomes an empty cup to be filled with whatever the teacher/interpreter wants. At that point the text becomes a homily of associations that are totally external to the text.

For example, when Jews speak of "crossing the Jordan River," it simply means that we actually cross from one side of a physical river to the other side as in the days of Joshua the son of Nun. This phrase has associations with the children of Israel entering the Promised Land. On the other hand, many Christians sing about crossing the Jordan and "going to the Promised Land" as a metaphor for dying. This association comes not from the Bible, but from pagan Greek mythology that says a dead person has to cross the River Styx and "go to the other side." By associating the Biblical text with an external pagan myth, they made an associative allegory that has nothing to do with crossing the Jordan River.

Once when I was in high school in America, a teacher asked the students in chapel, "What does Jesus mean to you?" It was a very good question, and different students gave different answers. One student raised his hand and said, "Jesus means to me my dog Rover." Everyone began to laugh! When I thought about this event many years later though, I realized that the student was very sincere. He loved his dog, and the dog comforted him. When he thought about Yeshua and how Yeshua comforts him, or relates to him, he associates that relationship with the one he had with his beloved dog Rover. That was his private and personal association, and there is nothing wrong with that.

The problem begins when people start associating with no rules because then it can become a limitless exercise. This idea of association, the "*drash*" part, has to have rules and reasons. One cannot simply go wild and rip things out of context to make a text say whatever he wants.

A few years ago I spoke in a church, and we went to the pastor's house afterwards with all the elders for coffee and cake. I was rather shocked when one of the elders said, "I'm so happy that Israel is the wife of God and that the Church is the wife of Yeshua."

I did not know how to respond, so I said, "That is an interesting idea, but it means that we cannot be brothers! Both of us believe in Yeshua, but if we have different mothers and fathers we can only be cousins."

Then he opened his Bible and read a text from the book of Leviticus and said, "See here, there were two barley cakes anointed with oil offered on the Sabbath day. One is Israel, and one is the Church."

I asked him, "How did you get this from this text? Where does it say one cake is Israel, and one is the Church?"

The elder very calmly replied, "Only spiritual people can understand spiritual things."

This sort of problem happens all the time, and people want to talk about the "spiritual meaning" of the text. In truth, using the levels of PARDES may lead to some good "spiritual" conclusions and interpretations, but they have to make sense with the literal textual meaning as well. There are four types of understanding that exist, but they cannot be applied wildly or without rules.

The Jewish Mindset of the New Testament

In **Romans 3:1-2**, Paul asks, "*What advantage does the Jew have? Or what is the value of circumcision? Much in every way! To begin with, the Jews were entrusted with the oracles of God.*" Even today the Scriptures belong to Israel because both the Old and New Testaments are Jewish texts. If the Holy

Sprit, speaking through Paul, says, "God gave them the texts," it is time for the Church to learn the Scriptures through the eyes of the Jewish people, through the historical context in which the Scriptures were created, and in their original language. The language of the New Testament is Jewish! When Greek people read the gospels, they think they are written in terrible Greek. Much of the New Testament Koine Greek contains Hebrew idioms that were simply written in the Greek language. It is Greek language with a Hebrew mind.

There are phrases in the Gospels that make no sense in Greek because they come from Hebrew. **Luke 9:51** says, for example, *"Yeshua turned his face toward Jerusalem."* This is not a Greek expression at all, and a Greek speaker could totally misunderstand what it means because in Greek it literally says, "He took his face and turned it toward Jerusalem." That sounds as though Yeshua twisted His neck around and turned His face towards Jerusalem so He could see in that direction. This expression is actually what is called a "Hebraism" though, which means He started going in the direction of Jerusalem. Only by applying a Jewish hermeneutic to these Jewish texts is it possible to explain some of their textual problems.

Inspiration and Scripture

One more concept that has to be addressed here is one of the most complicated and controversial, and this is the idea of "inspiration." **1 Timothy 3:16** says without hesitation, *"All scripture is inspired by God…"* Clearly the text is inspired, but then one has to ask, "What does "inspired" mean, and how was it inspired?

The traditional fundamentalist view both in Judaism and in Christianity is that God dictated the text to the writers. This highly conservative view of inspiration says that every word in the Bible is from God. This creates a problem because the original manuscripts no longer exist. No one living today has ever seen the text that Moses wrote or anything with Isaiah's original handwriting or Paul's original letter to Corinth. Those who believe in the dictation theory have to believe that the ultimate inspired text is the "original autograph" that the writers received from God. The problem is that none of the ancient texts were written in English or German or Portuguese, so the Bible that most people read in their native languages cannot be "inspired" according to this understanding. Most languages have multiple Bible translations, so which one did God inspire? This creates a difficulty.

In other words, the whole dictation theory is problematic because no one has those original scrolls, tablets, or papyri. Nobody has them; nobody has seen them. There is nothing with which to compare them.

What really happened in the writing of the Bible is completely different. What we have today is **a record of the inspired events**. There were reliable eyewitnesses who saw what happened and reported it. **2 Peter 1:16-18** says, *"For we did not follow cleverly devised myths when we made known to you the coming of our Lord Yeshua the Messiah, but we were eyewitnesses of his majesty... We ourselves heard this very voice borne from heaven, for we were with him on the holy mountain."*

The Bible is an inspired record for several reasons. First, the events themselves were inspired by God. They are the record of the works that God did among men. God did these works, and men witnessed them. Then those men wrote them down correctly, according to their view of what they saw and what they experienced. When they wrote it, the Holy Spirit gave it a "stamp of approval" so to speak by allowing the

Church to confirm and use these records as authoritative. In my opinion, that is how inspiration works.

This is important because we cannot ignore the fact that there are a number of problems in the Biblical texts. The Bible contains four gospels, so it is important to ask ourselves why. One gospel would have been enough, and three of them are synoptic, which means they tell the same basic story. Nevertheless, these three synoptic gospels sometimes differ from one another in the details they recount and the words they use. They each tell the story from their own angle. To add to the confusion, the Gospel of John has all the stories in a completely different order and with a totally different emphasis. If they were dictated by God, then God should have dictated one story, simple and true, and not caused all this confusion.

The fundamentalist view of inspiration is simply not logical. It is much more logical to believe that the Bible is a record of God's inspired events that have been recorded by honest, true, and inspired men. This is a very different approach. The God of Israel works in history among human beings and helped those events be recorded for posterity. Since He worked through human beings, however, each person can witness and record the same event in a different manner. When somebody reports an event, he interprets it from his point of view.

I know how this works from my relationship with my wife. We can go to the same places and have the same experience. We can eat in the same restaurant and speak with the same people, but when she tells the story, it sounds completely different from when I tell the story. When I tell the story, she always corrects me because we are different people. Each one of us brings our own baggage to that event, and different aspects of what happened there are more important to me than the points that stood out to her.

That is the reason why there are four gospels in the New Testament. The "synoptic problem" does not only exist in the New Testament though. The Tanach also contains several synoptic books. For example, the books of Exodus, Leviticus, and Numbers are synoptic with the book of Deuteronomy. The Books of Samuel and Kings are parallel to the Books of Chronicles. Isaiah chapters 6-37 are parallel to II Kings from chapter 8 to the end. There are many other examples of synoptic accounts in the Bible. This principle not only applies to historical books but also to visions and dreams that the prophets had. When a prophet says, "I saw a vision in which the Lord said to me…," I accept that his quotation of the Lord in the vision is a dictation. Sometimes, however, even cases like that can be handed down as synoptic texts. For example, Isaiah 2 is parallel to Micah 4, but there are still some differences. God spoke to Isaiah, and He spoke to Micah. Almost all the words in these texts are the same.

One especially interesting example of synoptic texts even comes from the most inspired text that God spoke and everybody heard. All of the people of Israel heard the Ten Commandments. God spoke to them from the mountain, and everybody heard it. Yet somehow there are two synoptic records of the Ten Commandments in the Torah, one in Exodus 20 and the other in Deuteronomy 5. The classic illustration here comes from the commandment concerning Shabbat that appears in **Exodus 20:8** and in **Deuteronomy 5:12**. Exodus says, *"**Remember** the Shabbat to sanctify it,"* whereas Deuteronomy says, *"**Keep** the Shabbat to sanctify it."* Remembering is not the same as keeping, so what did God really say? This is the most dictated text of all the texts in the

Bible. It begins with the words, "*These are the words which God spoke.*" Some people would say that maybe Moses became a little bit older and forgot exactly what God said, while others would say that a totally different person in a much later time period wrote Deuteronomy. One traditional Jewish solution to this problem is to say that God miraculously said "remember" and "keep" at exactly the same time, which is one reason for lighting two candles on Erev Shabbat- one for "remember" and one for "keep."

If one continues to examine both texts, the commandment of the Shabbat in the book of Deuteronomy is longer than in the book of Exodus. In addition, the reasons for keeping the Shabbat are different. Deuteronomy says the reason to keep Shabbat is because the Israelites were slaves in Egypt, but Exodus does not say that at all. What did God really say?

No matter how one resolves these questions, one cannot deny that these are very serious issues. We base our lives on what is written in the Bible. People want to kill me in Israel because of what is written in the Bible! I have suffered a lot because I believe that Yeshua is the Messiah because of what is written in the Bible! Many days and hours of our lives are spent in study, teaching, praise, singing, and prayer because of it. Therefore, we have to take the Bible very seriously.

These kinds of problems prove that inspiration is not dictation but rather a record. God did not use the prophets as robots or typewriters, but when God spoke they repeated what He said within the character of the individual prophet, according to their own styles and viewpoints. God expressed His feelings, and the Bible is the correct expression of His feelings and opinions. This is one of the differences between the Greek and Middle Eastern definitions and views of truth. In the Western or Greek view, truth is only the facts, but the

Biblical and Middle Eastern definition of truth includes not only the facts, but also the feelings. Feelings are just as much truth as facts. Here is a demonstration.

"Two weeks ago I had a car wreck at 1:25 pm exactly. I was driving my car down the hill on Gaza Street. I stopped at the red light, and I was going to turn left. A car came from the other side and ran into me while he was going 80 kilometers per hour. He hit my car in the back and broke the wishbone/ axle in the back of my car. There were two children in the car and an American friend sitting beside me. The car spun and stopped in the middle of the street."

This really happened, and those are the facts. That is how it was recorded for the insurance report, but that was not all the truth. That account does not say how I felt or what emotions I experienced during that event.

If I told you the same story like a typical Israeli, it would sound like this: "I was driving peacefully home and taking some children from the congregation back to their homes after the service. I was minding my own business. I stopped at the red light, and then when the light turned green, I started driving in the direction of my friends' house. All of a sudden, like a demon, like a devil, this guy started racing toward me from the other side. He didn't look or see anything! He didn't care if he killed me! He ran right into me! The car turned, and I didn't know if I was going right or left because it came at me as a total surprise. The devil himself attacked me!"

This is the same story, except that in one version I used the German engineer model, and in the second I was a typical Middle Eastern Jew. Which one communicated more?

The facts are true, but there is more to the Biblical text than facts. God's Word is supposed to evoke feelings in us. In order to do that, it sometimes uses different techniques.

The language of the Middle East sometimes sounds like an exaggeration. "All of Galilee came to hear Him" is not strictly true; it is an exaggeration. There was probably at least one old grandmother who did not come to hear Him. If there was at least one person who did not go, then not all of the Galilee came to hear Yeshua. The Bible is a Middle Eastern Jewish document. Therefore, it must be understood in those terms. "All" is not always "every single person." It means a representative majority. There are many such examples, and this will become clearer further on.

Once again, the definition of "inspiration" according to the Jewish understanding is *"The record of the inspired events of God, recorded by inspired men."* This helps when confronting a problem in the text because it means that every little issue does not have to shake a person up and make him lose his faith.

One of the best examples is Stephen. He was an inspired man who was close to God. He was a servant of God and one of the deacons who was appointed to feed the Hellenistic Jewish widows and orphans. He was a man full of the Holy Spirit, but he made mistakes. For example, in his speech in **Acts 7:16**, he said that Abraham bought a cave to bury his dead in Shechem. The text of Genesis clearly teaches, however, that Abraham bought a cave in Hebron, not in Shechem, and they are not the same place. So is this text inspired or not inspired? It was inspired! It recorded Stephen's words. The Holy Spirit recorded what he said through the ears of those who heard him, and they recorded the truth. Stephen made a mistake, but the record is true. This is a very important point.

Acts 7:14 records another mistake Stephen made in his speech. He said that 75 souls went down to Egypt, but **Exodus 1:5** says 70 persons went to Egypt. That is what Stephen really said, and an inspired man gave a true record of what he said. What is inspired here is the record of Stephen's speech and how he gave it.

When the Gospels or the Books of Chronicles and Kings record two different accounts of the same event, one does not have to presuppose a "synoptic problem." Different people wrote about what they saw and heard from their own different viewpoints, which is a perfectly natural human phenomenon. God's purpose in allowing both texts to exist is to teach things that are not written in the *p'shat* through the comparison of the two texts, the *drash* method. Associating the two texts allows an understanding of something new that is not explicitly written in either text. Putting all these elements together is like taking flour, water, eggs, and butter and putting them together to make a cake. Although all of those ingredients can be eaten separately, they will not taste nearly as good as a cake. Using only the *p'shat* is a bit like eating the butter by itself, but God allowed all the synoptic texts and the problems found within them to exist so that the reader would be able to make an interpretive "cake" that tastes very good once put together.

Unusual Textual Features as a Catalyst for *Midrash*

One unavoidable issue when discussing synoptic accounts is the problem of apparent "errors" and strange features in the text, but all of them have a reason for being there. **Numbers 10:35** records the words the Israelites used to say whenever the Ark of the Covenant would travel. Today Jews all over the world say these same words whenever the Torah scroll is removed from each synagogue's ark each time it is read publicly. *"Rise up O Lord! Let your enemies be scattered, and let those who hate you flee before you."* What is unusual about this verse can only be spotted by examining the Hebrew text itself, however.

When one reads this verse either from a printed Hebrew Bible or from a Torah scroll, one feature immediately stands out. The text contains two upside down *nuns*, (the Hebrew equivalent of the letter "n"), which are larger than all of the other letters. These *nuns* frame the verse but are not attached to any word. The questions obviously arise of how one could translate this strange phenomenon and why it is there.

Any German engineer who sees this would say it is an error because that is what it looks like on the surface, and it does not have an obvious purpose. On the other hand, a rabbi who sees the same feature would say, "What does God want to teach us from this strange thing? Everything has a reason." Scribes have been copying this text by hand for thousands of years with these upside down *nuns* and have not taken it upon themselves to "fix the mistake" there because the existence of those *nuns* is simply an invitation for a *midrash*. To a rabbi, any textual "problem" is an invitation for a *midrash*.

These kinds of *midrashic* opportunities are also taken by the New Testament writers when they are interacting with texts from the Torah. **Hebrews 11:4** says, "*By faith, Abel offered to God a more excellent sacrifice than Cain, through which he obtained witness that he was righteous, God testifying of his gift; and through it he being dead still speaks.*" How does the writer of Hebrews know that? According to **Genesis 4:8**, "*Now Cain said to Abel his brother; and it came to pass, when they were in the field, that Cain rose up against Abel his brother and killed him.*" This verse, as it stands in the Masoretic text, is missing something because it never records what Cain said to Abel. This missing information is an invitation for a *midrash* because usually the text would indicate what was spoken between the two brothers. This gap led many different Jewish commentators to speculate about what their conversation was.

Philo of Alexandria said they had a philosophical argument, and other Jewish interpreters said they argued about to whom the earth and the air belonged. Another Rabbinic interpretation says that Cain and Abel discussed whose sacrifice was better, which seems to be the view that Hebrews takes.

There are sometimes mechanical problems with the letters in the text too that seem to jump out and say, "Explain this." Whether there are unusual dots over the letters or letters that are printed larger than the other letters, a good rabbi says that it is not a mistake, but rather a part of the inspiration of the text. God gave these traditions as symbols so we would think deeply about what He is really saying to us. These are the kinds of things that cause a *midrash* to happen.

One other interesting textual abnormality occurs in **Isaiah 9:5-6** in the famous passage about the birth of the Messiah. It says, *"For unto us a son is born, unto us a son is given; and the government shall be upon his shoulders. And his name shall be called, 'Wonderful counselor, Mighty God, Father of Eternity, Prince of Peace.' There will be no end to the increase of his government or of peace on the throne of David and over his kingdom, to establish it and to uphold it with justice and righteousness from then on and forevermore. The zeal of the Lord of Hosts will accomplish this."*

What is unusual here in Isaiah 9 is that the word *"l'marbeh"* (to the increase) contains a **final** *mem*, (the Hebrew equivalent of the letter "m"), even though the *mem* occurs in the middle of the word and not at the end.[IV] In order to find out why there is a closed or a final *mem* in this word, the Rabbis tried to examine the context of the passage, which is clearly talking

---

IV   One thing that is essential in order to understand this concept is the rule that in Hebrew there are two kinds of *mems*, one kind which is "open" and can occur at the beginning or in the middle of a word, and one kind which is "closed" and only occurs at the end of words.

about the Messiah and redemption. The Radak (Rabbi David Kimchi) wrote comparing this closed *mem* in the middle of the word to a place in **Ezra-Nehemiah 2:13** where there is an open *mem* at the end of a word in a passage talking about the walls of Jerusalem being broken down. He said, "*Lamarbeh ha-misrah- To the increase of his power:* the *mem* is written closed, although it should be read as an open *mem.* The opposite thing happens in Ezra-[Nehemiah] in the *mem* of *lahem p'rutzim,* (they were broken down), in which the *mem* at the end of the word is written open. There is a *drash* in this matter that when the walls of Jerusalem that have been broken down during the whole time of the Exile will be closed up, then in the time of salvation the broken places will be closed up and the power that has been closed up will be opened for the King Messiah."[V]

The Rabbinic explanation for this closed *mem* in the middle of a word, which only occurs once in the entire Bible, teaches that instead of a printing mistake, this text turns out to contain a *midrash*. In truth, it is the "problems" of the text that cause *midrash* to happen. In the Jewish view of inspiration, God continually uses the Bible, along with all its abnormalities, to cause us to understand His revelation.

Textual Families

One potential cause for some of this confusion is the existence of families of texts. The texts were copied by hand over hundreds of years, and each textual family had slightly different traditions for how to copy the text. The minor Talmudic tractate Soferim 37b tells a story about finding three Torah scrolls with minor variant readings in the Temple and what the sages did with those readings. "Three scrolls of the Torah were found in

V   Radak's comments on Isaiah 9:6.

the Temple court: the *Ma'on* scroll, the *Za'atutey* scroll, and the *Hu* scroll. In one of these, they found the expression of '*ma'on*,' and in the other two it was written, 'the Eternal God is *me'onah* (a dwelling place),' so they adopted the reading of the two scrolls and discarded that of the one scroll. In another of the scrolls, they found it written, 'And he sent the *za'atutey* (nobles) of the children of Israel,' and in the other two they found written 'and he sent *na'arey* (the young men of) the children of Israel,' so they retained the reading of the two and abandoned that of the one. In one of the scrolls, '*hu'* (he) was written eleven times, but in the other two '*hi'* (she) was written eleven times, so they adopted the reading of the two and discarded that of the one."[VI] Although all of these textual differences were minor, the sages still had to decide which scrolls had the "correct" and "official" reading.

In some cases, it would happen that one of these scribes found a different word and wrote it the margin, or other times, the scribe would miss a word and write it in the margin or in the tiny space between the lines of text. Then when another scribe was copying that scroll hundreds of years later, he had to decide whether to put those words back in the text where he thought they should be or whether to keep them in the margins. Anyone who looks at the original copies of the Dead Sea Scrolls can see that this problem happened very frequently. The texts from the Dead Sea Scrolls often prove to have originated in a different family of texts than that of the Septuagint or of the Masoretic text, (the officially accepted Biblical text within Judaism and most of Christianity as well). The oldest manuscript of a Masoretic text that is known today is only from the Tenth Century CE.

VI   English translation from *The Minor Tractates of the Talmud*. Ed. Rev. Dr. A. Cohen. Socino Press, 1971.

These differences within textual families sometimes cause interesting textual variants such as the one below. **Amos 9:11-12**, says, *"'On that day I will raise up the fallen tabernacle of David and repair its damages; I will raise up its ruins and rebuild it as in the days of old that they may possess the remnant of Edom and all the Gentiles who are called by My Name,' says the Lord who does this thing."*

On the other hand the text in, **Acts 15:16-18**, quotes these verses, and says, *"'After this I will return and will rebuild the fallen tabernacle of David. I will rebuild its ruins, and I will set it up so that the rest of **mankind** may seek the Lord, even all the Gentiles who are called by My name,' says the Lord who does all these things."*

The Masoretic (MSS) text of Amos says "the remnant of Edom," but then in Yaakov's quotation in the book of Acts it says, "The rest of **mankind**." The reason that this occurred is that the vowel signs were only added to the Biblical text much later by the Masoretes after the Seventh Century CE. Without vowel points, the word could either be read as *"adam"* (**mankind**) or *"Edom,"* so nobody made a mistake here. Since the text left an open door of ambiguity, Yaakov felt that he could approve the Gentiles coming into the fellowship of the saints without officially converting to Judaism and getting circumcised because it was God's prophetic promise. Exactly opposite of Yaakov's reading, however, the later Rabbis read the text to mean Edom instead of Adam because they used Edom as a code word to represent the evil Christian empire ruling over them from Rome. They could not openly speak out against Rome, so they made a *midrash* out of this text that referred to the eventual rule of the Jews over Edom, (the Roman empire).

By the way, the reason "Edom" refers to Christianity in Rabbinic literature is because the name of Esau (עשו) in Hebrew contains the same letters as the Hebrew word Yeshua (ישוע). Both of them contain the Hebrew letters *"ע = ayin," "ש = shin," and "ו = vav,"* but Esau is missing the letter *"י = yud,"* which symbolizes God/Lord and is the first letter of the "Tetragramaton." Therefore, when the Rabbis read about the restoration of the tabernacle of David, they tried to attack or reference the Church by calling it "Edom."

On the other hand, Yaakov quoted the Amos passage in a completely different context. There had been an argument about whether the Gentiles had to convert to Judaism before they could become followers of Yeshua or not, and Paul came to Jerusalem all the way from Asia Minor to represent the Gentiles. Peter and Yaakov were already in Jerusalem with the rest of the leaders, and they got into an argument. Contrary to what is taught in most universities and seminaries, a close examination of the text actually shows that Peter took Paul's side. It is popular to characterize Peter and Paul as constantly fighting with each other, but what Peter said in **Acts 15:10** was very reasonable. He said, *"Now, therefore, why do you put God to the test by placing upon the neck of the disciples a yoke which neither our fathers nor we have been able to bear?"* In fact, Acts shows that Paul kept completely quiet during this discussion.

Yaakov wanted to base the council's decision on a passage from the Prophets, so he quoted this passage from Amos, which says, *"Later I will restore the broken tabernacle of David, and his ruins I will rebuild."* Then verse 12 gives the reason for God making this promise as a way to gather and restore the rest of mankind. Verse 13 explains this further. The tabernacle of David was to be restored so that all the nations could come to salvation. This prophecy is not only for Israel, but also for the world. Yaakov argued his point by making a *midrash* according to his understanding of Amos. His reasoning is as follows: Since the prophets promised that the rebuilding of the tabernacle of David will include the Gentiles (the nations), let us not force the Gentiles now to take upon themselves the Law of Moses because it has already been promised by the Prophets. God has already taken responsibility for including them in His covenant, so we will only ask the Gentiles to do the minimum and keep the four laws given to Noah before the giving of the Torah on Mt. Sinai. These Noahide Laws say to abstain from idolatry, sexual immorality, bloodshed, and from eating blood. Since God had commanded Noah and his sons concerning these things, they apply to all of humanity because all humans descend from Noah. Yaakov derived his ruling by using his reasoning to interpret the passage in Amos.

Yaakov's method in Acts is called *halachic midrash,* "legal *midrash*," from which one can derive laws There is another kind of *midrash* called *midrash aggada*, which is based on stories, not legal material, and from it one derives theological teaching. While *halacha* means "to walk," or the practical outworking of our faith, *aggada* is a story or statement.

To summarize what I have just explained, the text of the Tanach was transmitted through different families of scribal traditions. Only three of these textual families survived. First, the Rabbis transmitted the Masoretic text, which is the standard Biblical text in the Jewish world today. Second, the Greek speaking world passed down the Biblical text by translating the Greek Septuagint from the Hebrew, and both the Syriac and the Latin Vulgate Bibles and their derivatives are based on this Greek textual tradition. The third textual tradition was only recently discovered when the Dead Sea Scrolls were found in 1948. There is also another textual family within the Samaritan tradition, but they only have the Torah and not the rest of the Bible. Each one of these traditions has some places where they read better than others. The reading of Amos in the Septuagint is better than the reading in the Masoretic text, but the Masoretic text is better in some places like Psalms 8, 16, and 22. Qumran is so new still that most people are not familiar with any alternate readings from the Dead Sea Scrolls.

Commands and Examples

Today we are all part of the Pharisaic revolution that says we can discover the will of God from the text of the Bible. Nevertheless, the text of the Bible contains different degrees of practical revelation. For example, "love one another" is a direct command, and there is no question about whether we have to obey it or not. Yeshua commanded His disciples, "Go into all nations and make disciples, teaching them to obey everything I have commanded you." This is also a command about which there can be no question. Direct commands do not usually require a *sod,* a *remez,* or a *midrash* in order to understand what they mean.

There are, however, other ways that God communicates to us from His Word. Sometimes He communicates through both positive and negative examples. By reading about what the early believers did, we can learn some important principles for today. Ananias and Saphira are negative examples in Acts that show us how not to behave, whereas Dorcas is a positive example of the importance of helping the poor and how God rewards those who take care of the needy.

One case of learning by positive example is the matter of tithing. There is no place in the entire Bible that commands tithing to one's congregation, yet most believers are firmly convinced that we are required to tithe. In the Tanach, God commanded the people to give a tithe to the Temple in Jerusalem in order to support the priests and Levites who served in the Temple. One might rightly ask how this commandment is related to a modern church or synagogue. The Temple no longer exists, and the pastor is not the High Priest. What right do modern pastors have to take something that had been designated for the Jewish people in context of the priests and Levites in Jerusalem and apply it today to their local congregations? How do we know that we are supposed to pay the pastor, the preacher, or the evangelist a salary?

Paul solved this problem in **1 Timothy 5:17-18** by making a *midrash* from the Torah. He said, "*Let the elders who rule well be considered worthy of double honor, especially those who work hard at teaching and preaching. For the Scripture says, 'you shall not muzzle the ox while he is threshing,' and 'the laborer is worthy of his wages.'*" His first proof-text is from **Deuteronomy 25:4**, and his second one comes from other verses in Deuteronomy that say an employer should not withhold his employee's wages. This is a classic *midrash*. Paul took verses from an agricultural context and applied them to someone working in the Body of Messiah. In other words, we take the needs that the congregation has, and we make a necessary inference. We learn through *midrashic* methods to justify the means and the actions. There are many examples of this, so let us complicate matters a bit.

When people today give money to their congregation, to whom does it go? In the Tanach, if someone had a lamb and wanted to give a gift to the Lord, he would bring it to the priest and burn it on the altar. The priest took his piece, and the rest of it got burned. Nevertheless, that lamb was given to the Lord. In the New Testament, Paul said that he was collecting money for the poor believers in Jerusalem. He never said it was supposed to be an offering for the Lord. In the Torah, however, when people gave money to the poor, it was still considered to a gift to the Lord. The Torah commanded the people to bring sacrifices and to give several different kinds of tithes. They had a tithe for the priests and Levites, and they also had to leave some of their crops in the field to feed the poor. The ancient Israelites had different kinds of giving, but the New Testament never gives a commandment to tithe. Therefore, in order for a pastor today to ask for a tithe, he must form *halacha* out of an example, rather than the commandment itself. Remember that *halacha* means "to walk," and we want to know how to walk out our faith in our everyday lives.

Besides the example of the Israelites giving money to the Temple, there are examples about giving in the New Testament that can be used to support the concept of tithing. **Romans 15:27** says, *"It pleased them, indeed, and they are their debtors. For if the Gentiles have been partakers of their spiritual things, their duty is also to minister to them in material things."* This verse essentially says that the non-Jewish believers should be so grateful for the spiritual blessing of knowing the Jewish Messiah that they are motivated to "give back" financially to the poor among the Jewish people. **1 Corinthians 16:1-2** says, *"Now concerning the collection for the saints, as I have given orders to the churches of Galatia, so you must do also. On the first day of the week let each one of you lay something aside, storing up as he may prosper, that there be no collections when I come."* Both of these examples deal with the same context in which Paul was raising money from his congregations to help the poor in Jerusalem. The only authority, therefore, by which today's pastors collect tithes is by taking an example of what the early believers did and applying it to today's situation.

There are many things that both the Church and the Jewish people do, which have not been directly commanded but which have been taken from an example in the Scriptures. One example is meeting together on the weekend. The New Testament never commands the church to meet every Sunday. There are only examples of believers meeting together. In **Acts 20:7**, we see that the disciples gathered together to meet on Saturday nights. *"Now on the first day of the week, when the disciples came together to break bread, Paul, ready to depart the next day, spoke to them and continued his message until midnight."* From this example then, Christians have developed a tradition to meet together on the first day of the Western week, which is Sunday. **Hebrews 10:25** instructs us not to neglect meeting together but never specifies how often those meetings should take place. Orthodox Jewish men meet together to pray two or three times every day based on the example of there being three daily offerings in the Temple. Christians, on the other hand, base the idea of a weekly Sunday meeting on the example of this passage from Acts 20.

Another current practice we take from Biblical examples is the question of what we do when we gather together. **Acts 2:42, 46** says, *"And they continually devoted themselves to the apostles' teaching and to fellowship, to the breaking of bread, and to prayer… And day by day continuing with one mind in the Temple and breaking bread from house to house, they were taking their meals together with gladness and sincerity of heart."* Based on this passage we pray, have fellowship, break bread, and study the words of the apostles together when we meet. We do not play bingo or have lotteries because we do not have any such command or example. Today's big fashion of having praise and worship with music, bands, dancers, and tambourines is not from the New Testament. In fact, the New

Testament only tells us to sing and never says anything about instruments at all. Today's fashion of using instruments is taken by example from texts in the Old Testament.

Another thing we do by example is to take communion together. Yeshua commanded His disciples on the evening of Passover and said, "Do this in remembrance of me," referring to the breaking of bread. He never said how often one should do it, but we know we should do it because He commanded it. This is why some churches today have communion every day, some once a week, some once a month, and others only once or twice a year. All we have are examples of how the early Church operated. The examples interpret the commandment. Examples constitute a simple *midrash*.

The difficulty comes today because we live in the 21st Century in a different culture, and we have different needs than they had in the First Century. We have to continue making *midrashim* and using Biblical examples to suit the needs of our own cultural context. In order to do this properly, we cannot ignore the Torah. A lot of people who oppose the Messianic faith and say, "We do not need the Torah," should give up asking their people for tithes because the only place that talks about tithes is in the Old Testament. If a person rejects the Torah, then he also should reject the principle of tithing. Why do so many Christians take praise and worship, tithes, and prosperity from the Old Testament when they reject the rest? It is hypocritical to say, "The Torah is finished and does not apply to us," and then pick and choose what we want from it before throwing away the rest. When Jews see what Christians pick and choose, it does not impress us.

Midrash Aggada

Let us now examine the concept of *midrash agadda*, the *midrash* that tells a story, in greater depth. **Hebrews 11**, the famous chapter of faith that tells the stories of the faithful children of God, is all based on *midrash agadda*. One classic example comes from verses 8 through 10. *"By faith, Abraham obeyed when he was called to go out to the place which he would receive as an inheritance. And he went out, not knowing where he was going. By faith he dwelt in the land of promise as in a foreign country, dwelling in tents with Isaac and Jacob, the heirs with him of the same promise. For he waited for the city which has foundations, whose builder and maker is God."* What made the writer of Hebrews think that Abraham did not want to inherit Jerusalem, Hebron, and Shechem the way God had instructed? God told him, "Go to the land that I will show you, and I will give you the land! Wherever you step will be yours!" Consequently, it is surprising when all of a sudden, according to Hebrews, Abraham was not even interested in the Land of Israel at all. The writer of Hebrews made the *midrash* that Abraham was interested in another country altogether based on his words to the sons of Heth in **Genesis 23:4** when he wanted to bury Sarah in Hebron. He said, *"I am a stranger and a sojourner among you"* and made it clear that he was not interested in owning any land in Israel except for the cave in which he wanted to bury his wife. What the writer of Hebrews says is not explicitly stated in the Torah, but he derives this idea from unexplained concepts that are written in the Torah.

This chapter has given some background regarding the concept of hermeneutics and the importance of using Jewish interpretive methods to understand difficult texts. We have used a lot of illustrations and examples of how people use different levels of interpretation all the time, explained the Jewish view of inspiration, and shown that synoptic accounts do not have to be a "problem." We have also discussed the concept of *midrash* and how both the Rabbis and the New Testament writers utilized this important interpretive tool. The rest of this book will deal more specifically with Jewish exegetical rules and focus on specific interpretive methods and principles in more detail.

Chapter 2:

The Major Jewish Rules of Interpretation of Scripture in the First Century

There are those who say they "believe only the Bible and nothing else." The problem with this idea, however, is that the Bible is a book, and it can only be understood by applying the normal rules of logic and language that are applicable to the interpretation of any literature. The truth is that the Bible contains many different kinds of literature, and each genre has its own rules of interpretation. One does not read a newspaper like reading poetry. One does not read a law book like he would read a personal letter or a novel. Time and place and circumstance affect the way all written texts are read and understood.

The Bible was written over a period of approximately 1000 years, and it contains words and parts written in several different Middle Eastern languages. Roughly forty different authors took part in the writing of the Biblical text. All of these issues complicate the matter of interpretation.

In the time of Yeshua, the Jewish world interpreted the Scriptures using seven major rules that were formulated by Hillel[VII] the Elder (60 BCE - 20 CE). Here is a short synopsis

---

VII   Hillel was the president of the Sanhedrin in Jerusalem in the last year of the first century BCE and through the year 16 CE. His partner in this position was Shamai. These two great men argued a great deal about everything, but together they left a deep mark on the world of Yeshua. In fact, what is called "The Golden Rule" (Matthew 7:12) was actually first formulated by Hillel who said: "What is hateful to you, do not do to your neighbor. This is the whole Torah and the commandments." (bShabbat 31a) Hillel handed his position down to his son Gamliel who was the Apostle Paul's teacher (Acts 5:34-39; 22:3).

of these seven rules with some examples from both the Tanach and the New Testament.

קל וחומר .1
Kal Vahomer
(Light and heavy or *a fortiori*)

Let us start with the first hermeneutical principle, known as *kal va-homer,* an argument described in Latin as *a fortiori*, or in English as "from the minor to the major." Although at first glance, this may be a confusing concept, it will become clearer as we examine it closely. The Scriptures are replete with this principle, so it is incumbent upon us to understand it.

One practical conclusion that can be drawn from the use of *kal va-homer* in general is the fact that there are different degrees of sin. This concept has been greatly misunderstood, but the Torah teaches the difference between "large" and "small" sins. Of course, God in His complete holiness cannot overlook any sin, but the Torah teaches which sins are more serious based on the punishment imposed for their violation. If the punishment is death, then one has committed a very serious sin. Committing a sin requiring the death penalty is obviously more serious than committing one for which the penalty is simply to sacrifice two pigeons.

For example, many Jews and non-Jews alike have the mistaken impression that if a Jew eats pork, he has committed a very serious sin. The reason modern Jews view eating pork in such a grave light is because it became an identity marker for membership in the Jewish community during times of persecution. On the other hand, although the Torah does forbid it, the only punishment for violating this prohibition is washing one's clothes and remaining unclean until evening, which prevented worship in the Temple or Tabernacle on that particular day. There is no sacrifice or payment required, and the following morning the person was pure again. Therefore, the Torah teaches that eating unclean food was not a very serious sin, compared to a lot of other prohibitions.

Yeshua, in fact, also teaches that some sins are more serious than others, as well as saying that some commandments are weightier than others. In **Matthew 5:17-20**, Yeshua says, "*Do not think that I have come to destroy the Law or the Prophets. I did not come to destroy but to fulfill. For assuredly, I say to you, till heaven and earth pass away, one jot or one tittle will by no means pass from the law till all is fulfilled. Whoever therefore breaks one of the least of these commandments, and teaches men so, shall be called least in the kingdom of heaven; but whoever does and teaches them, he shall be called great in the kingdom of heaven. For I say to you, that unless your righteousness exceeds the righteousness of the scribes and Pharisees, you will by no means enter the kingdom of heaven.*" This passage proves that there are lesser and greater commandments and lesser and greater sins. The same principle applies in understanding the concept of *midrash*. We learn about the big things from the small things.

The following passage further demonstrates how *kal vahomer* works. **Matthew 6:25-33** says, "*...Therefore I say to you, do not worry about your life, what you will eat or what you will drink; nor about your body, what you will put on. Is not life more than food and the body more than clothing? Look at the birds of the air, for they neither sow nor reap nor gather into barns; yet your heavenly Father feeds them. Are you not of more value than they? Which of you by worrying can add one cubit to his stature? So why do you worry about clothing? Consider the lilies of the field, how they grow: they* *neither toil nor spin, and yet I say to you that even Solomon in all his glory was not arrayed like one of these. Now if God so clothes the grass of the field, which today is, and tomorrow is thrown into the oven, will He not much more clothe you, O you of little faith? Therefore do not worry, saying, 'What shall we eat?' Or 'What shall we drink?' or 'What shall we wear?' For after all these things the Gentiles seek. For your heavenly Father knows that you need all these things. But seek first the kingdom of God and His righteousness, and all these things shall be added to you."*

This entire passage is a classic example of *kal va-homer*. If God takes care of the birds (the lesser), *how much more* will He also take care of human beings (the greater)? People are much more important to God than the birds, so if God feeds the birds and dresses the flowers of the field, then one can infer through *midrash* that He will certainly take care of humanity. Similarly, we are not to worry about what we wear. If we look at how God takes care of nature, He will certainly take care of man because man is the crown of nature!

The essence of *kal va-homer* is that if this minor commandment or principle is true, then it is obvious (*how much more?!*) that the major principle or commandment connected to it will be true, as well. Yeshua used this form of *midrash* over and over again in His teaching. Let us examine how Yeshua uses this principle in other places.

In **Luke 23: 28-31**, "*Yeshua turning to them, said, 'Daughters of Jerusalem, do not weep for Me, but weep for yourselves and for your children. For indeed the days are coming in which they will say, "Blessed are the barren, wombs that never bore, and breasts which never nursed!" Then they will begin to say to the mountains, "Fall on us!" and to the hills, "Cover us!" For if they do these things in the green* *wood, what will be done in the dry?'"*

The part of this example that fits the method of *kal va-homer* is the phrase, *"If they do these things to the green wood, what will happen to the dry wood?"* Although the precise phrase **how much the more** does not appear here, the logic is present in the comparison between the two types of wood. If terrible things occur in the midst of peace and prosperity, **how much more** will they happen during times of tumult and war? Something small is compared to something big, and conclusions are drawn from the thing that is small to the thing that is big.

Yeshua is also telling the young women of Jerusalem not to cry for Him but instead to cry for themselves and for Jerusalem. *How much more* shall they suffer if He is suffering? The "green tree" is a symbol of a righteous person. In **Psalm 1:3**, we see the example that the godly man *"shall be like a tree planted by the rivers of water."* **Psalm 92:12** also says, *"The righteous shall flourish like a palm tree."* In other words, the righteous person is equated with a green tree. Yeshua drew His analogy about the destruction of the green and the dry trees from **Ezekiel 20:47**, *"...Behold I am about to kindle a fire within you, and it shall consume every green tree in you as well as every dry tree; the blazing flame will not be quenched..."* Therefore, Yeshua was saying, "If I, as a righteous person must suffer, **how much more** will all of you evil people who are living in sin in this city of Jerusalem suffer?"

2 Peter 2:4-9 makes a similar point: *"For if God did not spare the angels who sinned, but cast them down to hell and delivered them into chains of darkness..., then the Lord knows how to deliver the godly out of temptations and to reserve the unjust for punishment for the day of judgment."* The implication is that if God can punish even the angels, who are greater in might and power than human beings, then He will certainly punish the evildoers among men, who are even more evil than the angels. (Peter similarly indicates that the godly can expect deliverance from temptation because of God's faithfulness; just as He is faithful to punish, He is also faithful to reward).

Within Jewish tradition, the use of *kal va-homer* to interpret the Torah's commands has resulted in the important *halachic* decision that a Jewish person who dies is buried on the same day if at all possible. The burial takes place as quickly as possible because of a *kal va-homer* interpretation of **Deuteronomy 21:22-23**. *"If a man has committed a sin deserving of death, and he is put to death, and you hang him on a tree, his body shall not remain overnight on the tree, but you shall surely bury him that day, so that you do not defile the land which the Lord your God is giving you as an inheritance; for he who is hanged is accursed by God."* We see from this passage that a criminal who has been executed by hanging should not have his body left on the tree overnight. He should be buried the same day. The sages maintained *kal va-homer:* if a criminal, *an evil person,* is not allowed to be desecrated and remain strung up over night without a proper burial, then *how much more* should somebody who is righteous and who is not a criminal, deserve to be buried quickly and honorably? This *halachah* is the reason why Yeshua was buried on the same day as His death and not allowed to hang on the cross overnight. This is a classic case of using *kal va-homer* to make a legal ruling from a *midrash*.

The principle of *kal va-homer* is very important in Western society too, though we may not have been aware of its origin. In particular, lawyers use it when they need to make a strong point in court. It is also a very significant hermeneutical principle for understanding the mechanics of *midrash*.

גזרה שוה 2.
G'zerah Shavah
(Equivocal expressions- Lit. "equal cut")

G'zerah Shavah is "the application to one subject of a rule already known to apply to another, on the strength of a common expression used in connection with both in the Scriptures." VIII In other words, once one finds a similar word, phrase, or root in two different passages, an analogy can be made between them. Making this analogy allows the interpreter to apply the same principles, conclusions, and applications to both of the texts and situations. *G'zerah shavah* is especially useful for making *halacha* if the situation in one of the texts is very clear but not in the other text. The same *halacha* will then apply to both situations based on the similar words or expressions. Even a cursory look at the Talmud reveals numerous discussions in which the Rabbis use *g'zerah shavah* to establish *halacha* in uncertain situations.

In the book of **Hebrews 3:6-4:13**, the writer compares equivocal expressions in **Psalm 95:7-11** and **Genesis 2:2** to make his point. These similar expressions are the words "works," "rest," and "day"/"today," and the fact that both passages contain these phrases means that the ideas within the verses can be applied to one another. The writer of Hebrews uses *g'zerah shavah* to draw attention to the pattern of the work of God's creation and history. The entire analogy is based on the use of the word "day" or "today" (היום). *"...But encourage one another as long as it is called "today," lest any one of you be hardened by the deceitfulness of sin. For we have become partakers of Messiah, if we hold fast the beginning of our*

VIII   *The Babylonian Talmud: Glossary.* Ed. I. Epstein. Index Volume. London: Socino Press, 1952, p. 734.

assurance firm until the end, while it is said, 'Today if you hear his voice, do not harden your hearts, as when they provoked me…" (**Heb. 3:13-15**). (This is a short excerpt of the passage, but a complete reading of Hebrews 3-4 is recommended for a better understanding). The writer intimates that "today" carries two significant implications, which are a beginning and an end. By drawing from Psalms 95 and from the story of Creation, he concludes that there is a future Shabbat that we are all awaiting. This concept, which is also found in Rabbinic writings and other Jewish books from the Second Temple period, is that history will be 6000 years long, and the seven thousandth year will be a "Sabbatical year"- the Messianic Age. Therefore, we ought to take the opportunity now while it is "today" to repent and walk in faithfulness and obedience to Yeshua.

Another example that is often cited is the quotation from Hosea the prophet that Matthew uses in the birth narrative: "*out of Egypt have I called* my *son*" (**Hosea 11:1**). Since "Egypt" is mentioned in both cases, there is a connection and a similarity between the Exodus from Egypt and Yeshua coming out of Egypt with Joseph and Mary after Herod's death.

3. בנין אב מכתוב אחד
Binyan av mikatuv echad
(Making up a "family" from one text)

The essential meaning of *binyan av mikatuv echad* is that when an idea is found in several different passages, one can draw conclusions from the cumulative effect of putting them together.

Risto Santala explains this principle as the "classification of Bible verses, opinions, and facts into one family. In *midrashic* literature, there may be in one chapter as many as a hundred different Bible passages. It was sufficient for one to mention only the beginning of the verse and the word '*va-gomer,*' that is, 'and it continues,' and each person would repeat the whole verse in his mind… In addition, it was allowed *to borrow only the main idea of the verse* or *combine* in the name of a prophet ideas belonging to the same 'family,' slightly modified into its own unit."[IX] One may not combine verses using this method based on the fact that both of them contain a common word such as "then" or "kill" for example, and the word or phrase that connects the "family" of texts must be the primary idea within all those verses.

For example, **Hebrews 9:11-22** applies the ideas of "blood" from sacrificial and covenantal contexts in the Torah (such as Exodus 24:6-8, Lev. 8:15-19, 17:11, 16:14-16, and Num. 19:4-18 among others) and the idea of "covenant" in **Jeremiah 31:31-34** to its discussion of how Yeshua's death atoned for our sins. The writer of the book of Hebrews connects the blood of the sacrifices with the establishing of a covenant through the blood that Yeshua shed. He then connects the whole issue of blood with the New Covenant.

*"For if the **blood** of goats and bulls and the ashes of a heifer sprinkling those who have been defiled sanctify for the cleansing of the flesh, **how much more** [this is a clear kal va-homer] will the **blood** of the Messiah, who through the eternal Spirit offered Himself without blemish to God, cleanse your conscience from dead works to serve the living God? For this reason He is the mediator of a **new covenant**, so that, since a death has taken place for the redemption of the transgressions that were committed under the first **covenant**, those who have been called may receive the promise of the eternal inheritance.*

IX   Santala, Risto. *Paul, the Man and the Teacher in the Light of Jewish Sources.* Jerusalem: Keren Meshichit, 1995.

*For where a **covenant** is, there must of necessity be the death of the one who made it. For a **covenant** is valid only when men are dead, for it is never in force while the one who made it lives. Therefore even the first **covenant** was not inaugurated without **blood**. For when every commandment had been spoken by Moses to all the people according to the Law, he took the **blood** of the calves and the goats, with water and scarlet wool and hyssop, and sprinkled both the book itself and all the people, saying, 'This is the **blood of the covenant** which God commanded you.' And in the same way he sprinkled both the tabernacle and all the vessels of the ministry with the **blood.** And according to the Law, one may almost say, **all things are cleansed with blood**, **and without shedding of blood there is no forgiveness**.*" (**Heb. 9:13-22**)

The writer's conclusion from combining all these texts together is that *"Without the shedding of blood there is no forgiveness"* in the covenantal relationship between God and the people and that, therefore, Yeshua's sacrifice of Himself allowed our sins to be forgiven and for us to enter the New Covenant. There is no place in the Tanach that actually says sins are only forgiven with blood sacrifices. Instead, this idea is the conclusion of the writer which he draws from the application of one place that speaks of blood as atonement in a covenant situation to other places that speak of blood. This is a clear example of how a "family" is made up of one text with the emphasis on one or two words.

בנין אב משני כתובים .4
Binyan av mish'nei ketuvim

(Making up a "family" from two or more texts)

This is similar to the previous principle of *binyan av mikatuv echad*. The difference is that the application comes from combining two different texts and then applying the concepts in both to a "family" of other passages.

Let us use another passage from Hebrews as an example of how this works, although there are many other places in the New Testament that use it as well. **Hebrews 1:5-14** uses this principle to prove that the Messiah was greater than the angels. He combines the texts of **Psalm 2:7** and **2 Samuel 7:14** and then puts them together with a lot of other psalms with a Messianic context.

"For to which of the angels did He ever say: 'You are My Son, Today I have begotten You'? [Psalm 2:7] And again: 'I will be to Him a Father, and He shall be to Me a Son'? [2 Samuel 7:14] But when He again brings the firstborn into the world, He says: 'Let all the angels of God worship Him.' [Psalm 97:7] And of the angels He says: 'Who makes His angels spirits and His ministers a flame of fire.' [Psalm 104:4] But to the Son He says: 'Your throne, O God, is forever and ever; a scepter of righteousness is the scepter of Your kingdom. You have loved righteousness and hated lawlessness; therefore God, Your God, has anointed You with the oil of gladness more than Your companions.' [Psalm 45:6-7] And: 'You, LORD, in the beginning laid the foundation of the earth, and the heavens are the work of Your hands. They will perish, but You remain; and they will all grow old like a garment. Like a cloak You will fold them up, and they will be changed. But You are the same, and Your years will not fail.' [Psalm 102:25-27] But to which

of the angels has He ever said: 'Sit at My right hand, till I make Your enemies Your footstool'? [Psalms 110:1] Are they not all ministering spirits sent forth to minister for those who will inherit salvation?"

In this chain of texts in Hebrews 1, the writer uses both *binyan av mikatuv echad* and *binyan av mish'nei ketuvim* in a useful way in order to identify Biblical principles and prove that Yeshua is superior to the angels. The writer makes many verses that have nothing to do with one another relevant to his situation by application of the principle of "son" to all the texts that speak of God and angels that he lists to make his point. Bible teachers use this principle all the time when they build a sermon and connect different texts by associating one phrase or principle that appears in the main text to the other texts and then drawing a conclusion.

5. כלל ופרט
K'lal Uf'rat
(general to the particular)

In *k'lal uf'rat,* a major principle is stated and then expanded and listed below into greater detail. At times this principle works in the opposite direction too, meaning that one reasons from the particular to the general. In this second option, פרט וכלל *(frat uk'lal),* one initially has the details and then creates a principle at the end out of the details.

2 Cor. 6:14-17 says, *"Do not be unequally yoked together with unbelievers. For what fellowship has righteousness with lawlessness? And what communion has light with darkness? And what accord has the Messiah with Belial? Or what part has a believer with an unbeliever? And what agreement has the temple of God with idols? For you are the temple of the living*

God. As God has said: 'I will dwell in them and walk among them. I will be their God, and they shall be My people.'"

"*Do not be unequally yoked together with unbelievers*" is the general principle. Then Paul expands and details this principle in a set of explanations about what the principle entails in the rest of the paragraph.

The Torah also uses this method in the list of the Feasts of Israel in **Leviticus 23:2ff**. Verses 2-6 say, *"Speak to the children of Israel, and say to them: 'The feasts of the LORD, which you shall proclaim to be holy convocations, these are My feasts. Six days shall work be done, but the seventh day is a Sabbath of solemn rest, a holy convocation. You shall do no work on it; it is the Sabbath of the LORD in all your dwellings. These are the feasts of the LORD, holy convocations which you shall proclaim at their appointed times. On the fourteenth day of the first month at twilight is the LORD'S Passover. And on the fifteenth day of the same month is the Feast of Unleavened Bread to the LORD; seven days you must eat unleavened bread...'"*

The general principle in this passage is the phrase, *"The feasts of the LORD, which you shall proclaim to be holy convocations, these are My feasts."* Then underneath this general principle follows a list of the feast, and how each of them ought to be observed.

כיוצא בו ממקום אחר **.6**
Kayotzei bo mimakom acher
(Analogy made from another passage)

In this principle, the expounder compares two passages that appear to contradict one another with a third passage that contains some of the same general ideas in order to resolve the apparent contradiction. Here are some examples:

There is a numerical disagreement between **2 Samuel 24:9** and **1 Chronicles 21:5** and their accounts of David's census. 2 Samuel says, *"...and there were in Israel 800,000 valiant men who drew the sword, and the men of Judah were 500,000 men."* On the other hand, in 1 Chronicles 21's account of the same census, it says, *"...and all Israel were 1,100,000 men who drew the sword; and Judah was 470,000 men who drew the sword."* Some critics might consider the incongruity between the two texts to be very serious because even if one does not expect numbers in an ancient text to be exact, one does expect reports of a census to be somewhat consistent with one another. It is only by closely reading **1 Chronicles 27:1-22**, however, that one can explain this numerical disagreement. This passage explains that two of the tribes (Gad and Issachar) were not even counted in this so-called "census." Most likely, the number in 2 Samuel does not include those tribes, but the total in 1 Chronicles 21 does include those tribes. It is only by examining the third text that the contradiction between the numbers can be resolved.

The rabbis use this principle in the Talmud with great frequency to resolve apparent contradictions in the Torah, and the New Testament does the same thing as well. **2 Peter 2:4-8** explains the apparent contradiction between two passages in the Tanach that talk about the Messiah as "the cornerstone." On the one hand, **Isaiah 28:16** seems to say that the "cornerstone" will be widely believed in and accepted, but on the other hand, **Psalm 118:22** says the cornerstone will be rejected. Peter resolves this contradiction by inserting another passage from **Isaiah 8:13-15** that mentions the disobedient "stumbling" over a stone but the righteous serving God faithfully.

Here is the passage: *"And coming to him as to a living stone, rejected by men, but choice and precious in the sight of God, you also, as living stones, are being built up as a spiritual house for a holy priesthood, to offer up spiritual sacrifices acceptable to God through Yeshua the Messiah. For this is contained in the Scripture, 'Behold, I lay in Zion a choice stone, a precious corner stone, and he who believes in him shall not be disappointed.' [Isaiah 28:16] This precious value then, is for you who believe, but for those who disbelieve, 'The stone which the builders rejected has become the chief cornerstone,' [Psalm 118:22] and 'A stone of stumbling and a rock of offense.' [Isaiah 8:14] For they stumble because they are disobedient to the word, and to this doom, they were also appointed."*

דבר הנלמד מעניינו .7
Davar ha-nilmad me-inyano
(Explanation obtained from context)

This rule is actually one of the most fundamentally important rules of Biblical interpretation. A text must be examined within its total context if it is to be understood properly. A great deal of Paul's teaching especially is either incomprehensible or subject to drastically wrong interpretations unless the general context is also considered. The book of Galatians is a great example of the importance of context for understanding the writings of the Apostles.

Another example is **Romans 14:1**, which says, *"I know and am convinced by the Lord Yeshua that nothing is unclean of itself; but to him who considers anything to be unclean, to him it is unclean."* If one ignores the general context of Paul's letter, one could come to the conclusion that Paul officially annulled all the dietary laws of the Torah. When the context of Paul's own life and the problem of unity between Jewish and non-Jewish believers in the congregations with which he is dealing is taken into account, however, it becomes clear that the meaning of this verse is not so simple. By looking at the rest of the context of Romans, we see that Paul teaches that nothing is intrinsically "unclean" but rather that things are only "unclean" because God called them "unclean" in the Torah. Each believer has to decide according to his own conscience through the guidance of the Holy Spirit and the Scriptures what is clean or unclean for himself.

The second contextual issue raised by Paul is that there is "freedom from criticism" on issues of food, holidays, and life style because the essence of "the Kingdom of God" is not really about these minor issues. These are also minor issues in the Torah itself, and they are certainly secondary to the salvation of the Gentiles and the Jews. What we eat should not become a stumbling block to the salvation of those around us. The context clearly defines the problem and upholds what Paul says in **Romans 3:30-31**: *"Since there is one God who will justify the circumcised by faith and the uncircumcised through faith. Do we then make void the law through faith? Certainly not! On the contrary, we establish the law."*

In my opinion, the seventh of all these principles of Hillel is the most important one because it is the one that is ignored and misused most of the time. The context of the matter is the main tool for understanding the issues and the principles that the writer intended for us to understand. If we ignore the context, we actually make the Word of God of no avail because it could be made to say anything, to justify anything, to be twisted into anything. In fact, it could become the most horrific tool of evil, as it unfortunately became in the hands of those who have misused it over the centuries.

It must be borne in mind that not every passage can be interpreted with all of these seven rules, and there may even be some passages that should not be interpreted with any of them. If understood and used properly, however, these principles or *midot* can become a great tool within the Body of Messiah for interpreting and expounding the Scriptures according to their original Jewish context. Hermeneutics, or the way we understand the Word of God, is one of the keys to both spiritual health and the unity of the people of God. If we are able to use the same tools, we ought to have the same results and come to a common understanding of what God intended for us to learn and to know about Himself and His people.

Chapter 3:

Hekkesh

Although it is not included in either Rabbi Ishmael's or Hillel's lists of exegetical principles, one important Rabbinic method of interpretation is called *hekkesh*. *Hekkesh* is an "analogy proving the law in respect of one thing applies also to another, either because both have some features in common or there is a Biblical intimation to the effect."[X] *Hekkesh* literally means "to take two stones and hit them together," which is a metaphor for comparing two verses that have similar language in order to learn something not previously known. Though this technique is slightly technical and complicated, it lends itself to some beautiful *midrashim* and is used extensively in the Scriptures.

Hekkesh is different from *gezerah shavah* (analogy) because in this form, one verse is applied to another. We learn something from one verse and apply it to another verse. In *hekkesh*, however, two verses are examined that have the same words, but one emerges with a completely new doctrine that is not stated by either one of the verses alone.

One example of the use of *hekkesh* in the New Testament occurs in **Matthew 5:27-28**, where Yeshua says, *"You have heard that it was said to those of old, 'You shall not commit adultery.' But I say to you that whoever looks upon a woman to lust for her has already committed adultery with her in his heart."* How could Yeshua say that if a man looks upon a woman with the intent of sexual immorality, he has already

---

X   *The Babylonian Talmud: Glossary*. Ed. I. Epstein. Index Volume.
       London: Socino Press, 1952, p. 736.

committed adultery? In fact, there are many Rabbinic passages that forbid lust on exactly the same principles. What is unique then about Yeshua's equation of lust and adultery here is that He supported this *halachic* ruling by His use of *hekkesh*. He combined two of the Ten Commandments "You shall not commit adultery" and "You shall not covet" from **Exodus 20** and "hit them together" to make the conclusion that the Torah's prohibition on adultery also includes broader sins than simply the physical act of having sexual relations with another man's wife.

Yeshua was able to combine those two commandments because the Septuagint's word for "covet" in the 10 commandments is the same Greek verb (*epithymeo*) that Yeshua uses in Matthew 5 for "lust."[XI] "In other words, Jesus reads the humanly unenforceable tenth commandment as if it matters as much as the other, more humanly enforceable commandments. In Matthean ethics, if one does not break the letter of the other commandments, but one *wants* to do so, one is guilty."[XII]

Yeshua, in effect, takes two verses, strikes them against each other, compares them, and makes a *hekkesh*. In so doing, He teaches something completely new from this- that adultery is not only the physical act, but also the intention. He concludes that the commandment, "*You shall not commit adultery*" not only means the act itself, but also the intention which arises in the heart and is committed with the eyes.

The entire Sermon on the Mount in which Yeshua says, "*You have heard that it was said..., but I say unto you...*" is based on this principle of *hekkesh*. Some believers mistakenly

XI   Allison, Dale C. *The Sermon on the Mount*.
         New York: Crossroad Publishing Company, 1999, p. 72.

XII Keener, Craig S. *A Commentary on the Gospel of Matthew*.
         Grand Rapids: Eerdman's, 1999, p. 187.

think that Yeshua's teaching in the Sermon on the Mount was intended to annul the Torah. Actually the phrase, 'You have heard that it was said... but I say unto you...," appears in Rabbinic literature as well. It means, "One may think this applies only literally in the simple (*p'shat*), but *I say to you*, that it should not be taken only literally because it has many more facets to it." These other facets include things one can learn by interpretations of the *remez, drash,* and *sod* elements of a text. One can only make these kinds of conclusions by studiously comparing the texts.

Here is another example of how Yeshua used *hekkesh*. **Matthew 5:38-42** says, *"You have heard that it was said, 'An eye for an eye and a tooth for a tooth.' But I tell you not to resist an evil person. But whoever slaps you on your right cheek, turn the other to him also. If anyone wants to sue you and take away your tunic, let him have your cloak also. And whoever compels you to go one mile, go with him two. Give to him who asks you, and from him who wants to borrow from you do not turn away."* In order to discover Yeshua's basis for this ruling, we need to examine the texts from which He made the *hekkesh*.

The Torah says, *"An eye for an eye and a tooth for a tooth..."* but leaves us the task of deciding what the implication of this law is. Normally speaking, if someone deliberately puts out the eye of another person, the victim would be inclined to kill the perpetrator. This is the normal human reaction. Contrary to our natural tendencies, however, the Torah teaches that the victim of even such a terrible crime may not take revenge or retaliate in a violent way. The victim *does* have the right to go to court and receive financial compensation for the loss. The Torah does not teach that it is permissible to kill the person. If he took out an eye, he will pay for an eye. If he took out a tooth, he will pay for a tooth. If he burns someone, he will pay for the burn. This command in the Torah means that the one who caused the victim to lose an eye or a tooth will pay the price of the eye, the price of a tooth, etc. If someone damages an individual accidentally, the law is applied, and the courts determine how much the eye is worth. Different eyes cost different prices depending on the person's age, profession, etc.

The reason we know the Torah does not literally teach to remove the perpetrator's eye comes from another verse that explains how this principle is to be interpreted. **Exodus 21:22-25** applies the principle of "an eye for an eye" to a particular situation and interprets it to mean "the perpetrator must pay financial compensation." *"If men fight, and hurt a woman with child, so that she gives birth prematurely, yet no harm follows, he shall surely be punished accordingly as the woman's husband imposes on him; and he shall pay as the judges determine. But if any harm follows, then you shall give life for life, eye for eye, tooth for tooth, hand for hand, foot for foot, burn for burn, wound for wound, stripe for stripe."*

Nevertheless, there is another text in the Torah that seems to take this principle quite literally. **Leviticus 24:19** says, *"If a man causes disfigurement of his neighbor, as he has done, so shall it be done to him."* It is stated clearly in this verse that if someone pulls his neighbor's tooth out, he should have his tooth pulled out as well. This is a completely different legal outcome.

Yeshua saw that there was a legal contradiction in the Torah. In one place, it says that one must pay according to the judgment determined by the courts. In another place, it says that the guilty man's eye must be taken out as recompense for the victim's eye that had been lost. To add to the complication, let us now examine a third text in **Lamentations 3:30,** which says something else completely. *"Let him give his cheek to the one who strikes him, and be full of reproach."*

We have a situation here in which three different inspired texts all give completely different instructions. One says if somebody causes their neighbor to lose an eye, then they must go to the court to determine reparations, and that will be the perpetrator's monetary fine. The other one says that we are to retaliate in kind. If someone does something to another person, the exact same thing should be done to the offender. Still another verse says that if somebody hits, turn the other cheek! How can it be that all these texts are inspired by the same God? The only way to understand these verses is to use *hekkesh,* that is "to hit one against the other" and make a completely new idea.

To understand why Yeshua said to turn the other cheek, we also need to remember the cultural context in which He was speaking. During the time the Gospel was written, the Land of Israel and the Jewish people suffered under Roman occupation. Yeshua lived all of His life under Roman occupation and the corrupt government of Herod and his family. The Romans basically did whatever they wanted with the people of Israel. They had laws which said that any Roman soldier could take any Israelite's coat, shirt, donkey, and equipment at a moment's notice and even take him for 24 hours as a servant! After 24 hours he had to be released, however. The law in Israel is still more or less the same. If the military needs a car, they have the right to take it. If they need a house, they have the right to take it, just as the situation was in the time of the Romans.

Now that we have examined all three of the relevant texts in their contexts, let us now see how Yeshua made a *hekkesh* with them in the Sermon on the Mount. Yeshua is not talking about a case of mutilation by accident. The person who hits wants to humiliate. Yeshua says that when someone intentionally hurts or embarrasses us, we should not respond with evil against evil. Allowing that person to "hit us on the other cheek" is the strong thing, not the weak thing, to do. If someone intends to embarrass us publicly by striking us in the face, we must not give in to his evil and respond in kind because that would show him that he has affected us. Instead, we must prove to him that he cannot affect us. We must show him that we are proud and strong enough to stand another strike on the face. Yeshua teaches this from taking the two verses in the Torah and striking them together with the verse in Lamentations.

Therefore, "turning the other cheek" and "going the second mile" is not a wild new law that cancels the Torah. Rather, Yeshua expounded the Torah using *midrashic* principles and *hekkesh.* He took several verses that dealt with the same issue, analyzed them, made an analogy, "hit them against one another," and made a new conclusion to keep the verses from contradicting one another.

Now let us see how it is possible to use the principle of *hekkesh* in our own day to understand the Bible. The first time we meet Bezalel Ben Uri is in **Exodus 31:2-3**. The text says, "*See, I have called by name Bezalel the son of Uri, the son of Hur, of the tribe of Judah. And I have filled him with the Spirit of God, in wisdom, in understanding, in knowledge, and in all manner of workmanship...*" This verse mentions four attributes or gifts given to Bezalel: wisdom, understanding, knowledge, and all manner of workmanship. **Exodus 35:31** uses the exact same words used to describe Bezalel. "*He has filled him with the Spirit of God, in wisdom and understanding, in knowledge nd all manner of workmanship...*"

Exodus 36:1 describes Bezalel using another interesting

term, which literally in Hebrew means "a wise heart." In traditional Rabbinic thinking, wisdom comes from the head, and emotions stem from the heart. According to Nachmanides, (the Ramban), these things are opposites, but Rashi solves the apparent contradiction by making a classic *hekkesh*. He said that "knowledge" was, in actuality, the Holy Spirit or *Ruach ha-Kodesh.*[XIII]

According to the New Testament, the purpose of the Holy Spirit is to "lead us into all truth," as **John 6:13** says, *"...when He, the Spirit of truth, has come, He will guide you into all truth."* Truth in Hebrew is "emet" (אמת), of which the first, middle, and last letters are the first, middle, and last letters of the Hebrew alphabet. In other words, the Holy Spirit gives us the ability to synthesize, and in this classic *hekkesh,* we are able to come up with two separate things and understand a third. Westerners who hear Middle Easterners speak often think we are exaggerating, but truth also includes the accompanying emotions. This concept sheds light on what Paul says in **2 Corinthians 3:6** about how God gave us the ability to be ministers of the New Covenant *"not of the letter, but of the Spirit, for the letter kills, but the Spirit gives life."* This example, like the two passages we reviewed in the Sermon on the Mount, is also a *hekkesh.*

Of course, *hekkesh* needs to be used carefully and with the guidance of the Holy Spirit because whatever new conclusions we make from "striking verses against one another" must not contradict the letter or the Spirit of the Word of God. Our understanding and use of this important concept is a great tool for interpreting and expounding the Bible according to its original Jewish context.

XIII   Ben Isaiah, Abraham and Benjamin Sharfman. *The Pentateuch with Rashi's Commentary: A Linear Translation into English*. Vol. 2. Exodus. Brooklyn: S. S. & R. Publishing Company, 1949, p. 394.

Part Two:

Contemporary Challenges for Messianic Judaism

Chapter 4:

Messianic Jewish Hermeneutics

Although it is easily possible to talk about the hermeneutics of the early Church or Second Temple period Judaism, there never has been a fully developed and articulated system of Biblical interpretation which is both Messianic and Jewish. This chapter will discuss the need for hermeneutics, review some important Jewish contributions, and then propose some initial guidelines for Biblical interpretation within the Messianic Jewish community.

Hermeneutics has been called both a science and an art. There are laws and rules for understanding a text which must take the time, place, context, speaker, audience, and cultural and religious background into consideration. Texts do not float in the wide space of nothingness. They always exist within the context of some setting, time, and the historical events which led to their creation. The trend in the early part of the twentieth century was to give an existential twist to the interpretation of the Bible. This took the Word of God out of its historical and cultural context and gave it a philosophical meaning. It is my intention to restore the understanding of the ways in which the Bible has historically been interpreted, in order to equip those who are serious students to delve further into its intricacies and relevance to our daily life.

For purposes of clarity, let us define hermeneutics. According to the *Oxford Dictionary of the Christian Church*, hermeneutics comes from a Greek word which means, "to interpret." It is described as "the science of the methods of exegesis. Whereas exegesis is usually the act of explaining a text, often in the case of sacred literature according to formally prescribed rules, hermeneutics is the science (or art) by which exegetical procedures are devised."[XIV] Hermeneutics is the way we establish rules for interpreting texts so that the reader can understand the writer's worldview and intended message.

One cannot simply "read" the Bible without simultaneously interpreting it, whether or not we realize it at the time. The Protestant idea of *sola Scriptura* without any accompanying interpretive traditions or guidelines may sound attractive, but it is, in fact, impossible. We all approach the text with our own preconceived ideas about what the text means based on what we have been taught by others. In many cases, these previous understandings can be helpful in guiding our interpretation, but we must never rely solely on what we think the text "should" say. Instead, we need to use the interpretive principles of hermeneutics to uncover what the text meant in its original cultural context and only then seek to apply it to our own circumstances.

The Jewish attitude toward the Biblical text is that each statement has seventy possible understandings and interpretations. In practice this principle allows a wide range of possibilities for understanding the same text without breaking the consensus. This does not mean that everything is permissible, but it does mean that there is a place to evaluate and consider different possibilities and options for interpreting the same text.

Although at first glance it may appear that the Rabbis interpreted the Bible without rhyme or reason, there are, in fact, very specific rules for forming *midrash* and for exegesis within Jewish tradition. Rabbi Hillel, who lived in the First

XIV   "Hermeneutics." *Oxford Dictionary of the Christian Church*. Ed. F. L. Cross. Oxford University Press, 1983, p. 641.

Century BCE, had seven rules for interpreting sacred texts. It must be remembered that these hermeneutical methods never exclude the *p'shat*, the plain, literary meaning. The *p'shat* alone, however, cannot show us all "Seventy faces of the Torah," so the other methods are also important tools for seeing the full depth and richness of God's Word. In the Second Century CE, there was a very famous rabbi in the Land of Israel named Rabbi Ishmael. He enumerated thirteen exegetical principles for the Bible, which are still accepted guidelines in Judaism today, and many of which are found throughout the New Testament.[XV]

In **Romans 3:1-2** the Apostle Paul asks, *"Then what advantage has the Jew? Or what is the benefit of circumcision? It is great in every respect. First of all, they were entrusted with the Scriptures of God."* The contribution of Jewish tradition to the understanding of the Scriptures can be divided into two major areas, which are the Biblical text itself and its simple exegesis. The Rabbis call this *davar Torah*, which is the regulation of the Torah. Understanding comes from the process of deductive thinking concerning the text. In Hebrew this is called *severa*. In other words, it refers to the interpretation deduced from the Scriptures by logical conclusions or, as we would say in the West, hermeneutical principles.

God gave the Biblical text to the Jewish people, but the Rabbis preserved it and made it understandable and readable for all generations. Yeshua said this very clearly in **Matthew 23:2**, when He gave the Pharisees the right to interpret the Scriptures because they *"sit on the seat of Moses."* Let us remember, with gratitude, the labors of the innumerable Jewish scholars who, as far back as the pre-Maccabean period, dedicated themselves to the *Masorah,* which is the codification of the

---

XV   See Appendix A for a list of Rabbi Ishmael's 13 *Midot.*

Biblical text including critical notes. Words, letters, dots, and marginal readings were all dutifully weighed and scrupulously determined by the Rabbis and Scribes of the Torah.

The full story of what codifying the Scriptural tradition entails can be read in the minor Talmudic tractate *Soferim*, which means "Scribes." This treatise deals with details such as the space between letters, the width and height of the scrolls, the capital and final letters, etc. Without the work of these scribes, we would not have the Word of God available to us today because we would not be able to understand the most basic language of the Bible. This tractate also discusses the qualifications for preparing the books, their respectful handling, and their sanctity. We must realize and be grateful for the fact that Yeshua and the Apostles would not have even had the books of Moses if it were not for the Rabbis who preserved them and protected them from corruption.

Rabbinic tradition gave the vowel signs to the Tanach which make it possible to read the Bible thousands of years after it was written. An English text composed only of consonants would be incomprehensible. If we saw the letters GD in a book, how could we know what they meant? They could mean GooD, GoD, GooDy, GuaDiayo, or even aGeD. The only way to distinguish their true meaning would be by understanding the context, which is not always easy. It is the Rabbinic Jewish tradition which determined the text of the Hebrew Bible and made it readable and understandable for the whole world. The Rabbis also developed the PARDES method of interpreting the Biblical text on different levels, which we discussed in more detail in chapter 1.

Another Rabbinic method of interpretation is *gematria,* a coded method that enables one to interpret the meaning behind some numbers. Although we have to be very cautious today in using this method, it was a well known phenomenon to the writers of the New Testament. Here is one example of the Rabbinic use of *gematria*. **Genesis 14:14** mentions the 318 "trained men" of Abraham. 318 is the numerical value of the name of Eliezer, Abraham's servant mentioned in **Genesis 15:2**. It seems hard to believe that this is pure coincidence. The Rabbis, therefore, connected the story of **Genesis 14:14** with Eliezer and concluded that Eliezer was the person who trained the servants of Abraham and made them like himself.

Rabbinic exegesis is often the key to understanding Paul. Only Paul's dependence on Rabbinic tradition can explain his view that the Torah was given by angels and not directly by God (**Gal. 3:19**) or his view that the Messiah was the rock who followed the Israelites and gave them water in the wilderness (**1 Cor. 10:4**).

The Rabbinic tradition of Biblical exegesis has indisputably contributed to the understanding of the Bible in the past. It is my firm conviction that when Christianity is restored to its foundations in the future, Rabbinic principles and attitudes towards the text will aid its return to true Biblical faith. The Jewish tradition of the Rabbis and their love and preservation of God's Word is a heroic and constant song of devotion and fidelity in which both Jews and Christians can have fellowship and experience the fullness of God's revelation. Only around the Word of God can believers find fellowship and communion that someday might bring salvation to all mankind.

I will now attempt to propose a hermeneutic for Messianic Jews, and for all people who would like to discover Biblical truth.

Here are some basic guidelines:

1. The Bible is the Word of God and should be treated as such.

2. The Bible is a very ancient document and should be treated as such.

3. The Bible was not written in English. It is important for us to remember that whenever we study a translation, we are already beginning with an interpretation.

4. The Bible is a Jewish document and should be treated as such.

5. The Bible contains different types of literature. Each genre needs to be discerned and treated with the appropriate linguistic tools.

6. The Bible reflects a historical reality which must be understood within that context.

7. The Bible, as God's Word, communicates God's will. There is a spiritual dimension to the Bible which entails more than the careful use of hermeneutical principles. The Bible is more than a series of words, sentences, and chapters. It is also more than literature.

8. One needs the guidance of the Holy Spirit along with the proper use of hermeneutics in order to fully understand the words and discern the spirit of the Word.

In my opinion, these guidelines are axiomatic. They ought to be the rules not only for Messianic Jews, but for everyone who would like to understand the Bible. In the modern West, some people have treated the Bible as an existential book of God, totally disregarding its historical, cultural, or linguistic boundaries. Unfortunately, there are also people who use the Rabbinic method to justify wild interpretations of Scripture. We have to be balanced in our approach. Let me state my opinion clearly: ***not everything Jewish or ancient is automatically right and good.*** Rabbis and Jewish interpretation have been wrong at times, and any use of Rabbinic methods should be made critically and to the degree that the Biblical texts demand, based on the time and culture of the people who wrote them. Nevertheless, to study the New Testament, which is a First Century Jewish document, and to ignore the traditions of interpretation and exegesis that were used at the time, is to miss a very important tool for understanding the Word of God.

These guidelines are important for the development of a specifically Messianic Jewish hermeneutic for the following reasons:

1. These principles put the New Testament back into the context in which it was written. There needs to be a consciousness that we are dealing with a Jewish book and a Jewish Savior. This will cause the student to seek the solution to textual problems within the world of Yeshua. We must not seek non-practical solutions. Furthermore, we must not live under the illusion that "faith" is simply a confession or emotion instead of an action oriented commitment. *"For as the body without the spirit is dead, so faith without works is dead also."* (**Yaakov 2:26**)

2. Biblical science often has a historical and philological approach, but it can lack understanding concerning the inspiration of the text. When we look at the New Testament in its historical context, we see its principles of interpretation reflect the traditional Jewish approach. This is called *"midrash."* A Messianic Jewish approach ought to incorporate a solid historical and philological approach to understanding the Scriptures **as well as** a firm faith in the integrity and inerrancy of the Biblical text.

3. A Messianic Jewish approach to hermeneutics ought to deal with the Biblical text according to the genre in which it was written. Every text has its own poetic, narrative, literary, discursive, rhetorical, and thematic structures, each requiring its own form of analysis. One does not deal with poetry in the same way as prose, and the reader who tries to do so may miss the fundamental message the writers were trying to communicate. Not every text is meant to be taken literally. This is especially true of apocalyptic literature. There are very special rules for dealing with this type of text. My conviction is that without a comprehensive knowledge of inter-testamental and First Century Judaism, it is impossible to correctly understand the full intention and nuances of the texts.

4. The study of the Bible ought not to be merely an intellectual or spiritual process. It needs to be practical as well and to lead the student to "all good works." This is the reason Paul wrote to Timothy that, *"All scripture is given by inspiration of God, and is profitable for doctrine, for reproof, for correction, for instruction in righteousness, that the man of God may be complete, thoroughly equipped for every good work"* (**2 Timothy 3:16-17**). Our attempt to understand the Bible must

bring us to "do the will of our Heavenly Father." Hermeneutics must be a tool not only for understanding but also for doing the work of God among men.

Messianic Jewish hermeneutics faces a double pronged challenge. On the one hand, we must endeavor to deal with the Biblical text in an objective and authentic way in order to truly understand it within its cultural and historical milieu. On the other hand, we must work to free the text from the encrusted tradition of two thousand years. Unyielding doctrinal positions are evident in both Jewish and Christian study which must be examined and, if found to be erroneous, rejected. There are some traditions that have come from the Greco-Roman world, and they have infiltrated both the Jewish and Christian study of hermeneutics. Messianic Jews will have to learn to recognize and deal with erroneous, imported interpretations while sifting for interpretive traditions that may actually be helpful. We have to work very hard to develop an original and historical approach to understanding the Bible.

One of our current challenges is to raise the level of Biblical and Jewish education among Messianic Jews. Education must be as important to us as it is to the non-Messianic Jewish community. If we wish to, on some level, emulate the Jewish community, we must learn from the good things in it.

In the final analysis, all believers are going to have to deal with the same hermeneutical principles and approach the Bible according to its cultural and historical integrity and identity, which is a First Century Jewish book. When this happens, I believe that unity and understanding will be the outcome. As believers in Yeshua, we ought to seek a practical outcome to our study of our sacred texts. As we seek to put God's Word into action, we need to remember a number of things.

First, we ought to have a clear understanding that we are saved by faith, through God's grace, **for the purpose of obedience to God's commandments**. *"Was not Abraham our father justified by works when he offered Isaac his son on the altar? Do you see that faith was working together with his works, and by works faith was made perfect?"* (**Yaakov 2:21-22**) To many of us, it sounds simplistic to state that we have to obey God's commandments. In truth, this area of hermeneutics is probably going to be the most controversial in the development of a Messianic Jewish hermeneutic. The question will arise, "Which commandments and when?" Since this is such an important issue that deserves a full treatment, we will address this question in more detail in another chapter of this book.

Second, we ought to imitate the good examples of holy people in Biblical history. If we want to honor God's will, we have to take the examples of the early Church seriously. The behavior of the early believers ought to have a direct bearing on what we do and how we do it in our practice today. If they took communion each week on the "first day of the week," we ought to seek to understand the reasons and meaning of this action and emulate them in doing what they did as much as possible.

Finally, we must be aware that the world has changed with the advent of the modern lifestyle of the West. We no longer live in an agrarian society. For this reason, we must learn from our hermeneutics as well as our reason in order to apply Biblical situations and principles to our own lives. This will, no doubt, require necessary inferences arrived at through strict, logical analysis of Biblical teachings, examples, and principles. One of the prime examples of current challenges that need to be met in this area is the role of women in the life and administration of the congregation. While we cannot ignore Paul's direct commands in **1 Timothy 2:10ff** or **1 Corinthians 14**, we must find venues and means by which the modern woman can find herself active and fulfilled in God's kingdom. All this must be done without breaking or annulling any explicit commands in God's Word.

In my opinion, hermeneutics in the 21st Century will be more pluralistic, by allowing a broader cultural expression of Biblical faith. In practical terms, this means that Messianic Jews must put **Romans 14:10-13** into practice in a much more deliberate way in our congregations. "...*Why do you judge your brother? Or why do you show contempt for your brother? For we shall all stand before the judgment seat of Messiah. For it is written: "'As I live," says the Lord, "every knee shall bow to Me, and every tongue shall confess to God."' So then each of us shall give account of himself to God. Therefore, let us not judge one another anymore, but rather resolve this, not to put a stumbling block or a cause to fall in our brother's way."*

In addition, the Christian denominations must do the same vis-à-vis Messianic Jews. There will be congregations whose interpretations will be very different from the Church and perhaps even from other Messianic Jewish congregations. These differences must celebrate the universal nature of the Messiah's Body and cultural diversity among His children. At the same time, effective hermeneutical application will serve to break down the walls of folklore that Satan has built up to divide and diminish the effectiveness of the universality of the message of salvation in Yeshua the Messiah.

The challenge of a Messianic Jewish hermeneutic is to rediscover the spirit and the practices of the New Testament Church in the 21st Century. The future of the effectiveness of the Body of Messiah in the world will depend on our ability to overcome the shackles of tradition and to return to a much more Biblical faith. It will also depend upon our ability to seek greater unity among those who claim faith in Yeshua the Messiah, irrespective of their cultural orientation. This unity and spirit will be greatly enhanced by a development of a more Jewish hermeneutic in both Messianic Jewish and Christian circles.

The Jewish mind works in practical terms, and it is critical that the Body of Messiah understand this in continuing to develop theology and hermeneutics. In sharing the Good News with the Jewish people, it is very important that Messianic Jews apply the principles of hermeneutics in preparing their messages. Jewish people are often intellectually discerning and do not feel any obligation to listen when someone explains principles that they have heard all their lives. The Jewish discourse has to integrate something interesting as well as spiritual. There has to be a moral imperative and a practical application from the teaching that can be applied in the community and within people's personal lives. This kind of message can only be taught if the text is taken in context, with the proper principles applied. Messianic Jews have to work very hard on the messages they bring to their listeners. It is important for us to develop a style and approach to teaching that is compatible with Jewish practice and firm Biblical truths.

Chapter 5:

The Matter of *Mitzvot*

In an earlier chapter, we briefly mentioned the issue of commandments and how to interpret and practice the many *mitzvot* we find in the Biblical text. Let us now address these issues in greater detail. It is of great importance for Messianic Jews today to make an orderly synthesis of our thoughts about and practice of God's commandments. Commandments are the clearest things to follow when we interpret them literally, though we have to remember that there are all kinds of different *mitzvot*. There are gender and time specific commandments and other kinds as well.

One interesting question with which we must deal is the matter of head coverings. Although I wear a *kippah* at weddings and funerals and at Shabbat services, I do not actually like to wear one. If I were to literally obey every word of the New Testament, I would not wear a *kippah* at all, especially when I pray, because **1 Corinthians 11:4** says men should not pray with their heads covered. Verse 5 in that same chapter says that women should cover their heads. Paul said these things on the basis of a *midrash halacha,* through which he made a ruling for all the congregations that women should cover their heads as a sign of submission to authority. Most of the modern Messianic movement is doing this backwards. Men wear *kippot*, and women do not cover their heads at all. In most of the Evangelical world, neither the men nor the women cover their heads, but they are stricter about men. In most churches, a man who comes in with a hat will be asked to remove it.

Could it be that this command was only meant for the specific time and situation of the Corinthian congregation, or was it a command for all times and places?

In order to find out which interpretation is correct, we need to ask ourselves what kind of commandment this is supposed to be. Is it a *mitzvah* that is connected to a certain cultural time, place, and context, or is it a command for all times, in all places, and under all circumstances? Not all commands are for all times and for all people. Some *mitzvot* are designated for specific times and places and specific genders or groups of people.

The Torah has many examples of *mitzvot* that are designated for specific groups of people. For example, men are commanded to be circumcised and to study the Torah. Some commandments, such as purification after childbirth, naturally only apply to women. There are commandments only for priests and Levites that do not apply to a regular Israelite. They apply only to the specific people to whom the commands were given. Likewise, there are some *mitzvot* directed to Gentiles and others directed to Israelites. For example, people who were not circumcised were not allowed to eat the Passover, even though they were a part of Israel. They came out of Egypt, and they could have even been Israelites. Nevertheless, they were not permitted to keep the Passover. During the 40 years that Israel was in the wilderness, they did not keep the Passover because all those born in the wilderness were not circumcised. When they crossed the Jordan River, the first thing they did was to have mass circumcision. All the men of Israel were circumcised in order to keep the Passover. This is one example of the fact that not all the commandments are for everybody.

The New Testament has commands that are meant for only one group of people, too. When **Ephesians 5** says,

"*Wives, submit to your husbands as to the Lord*," we are clearly reading a directive that is meant for women only. There are also commandments for elders, elders' wives, deacons, children, etc.

We must keep things like genre and intended audience in mind because this is a part of the hermeneutic. Hermeneutics is a way to determine what God has required of us. In other words, what does the text really say, and how do we apply this knowledge in our lives?

Midrash is part of this hermeneutical process. It is a search for solutions from the text of the Bible to questions that the text does not directly address. *Midrash* is born out of the problems that exist within the text as well as the contemporary needs of the believing community, which the text does not directly address. We all live in a different world than the one that existed when the Bible was written. One simple example is that we no longer live in a primarily agrarian culture, and many of the Bible's commands are meant for an agricultural society and context. The more technology our world invents, the more questions we have to answer about how God intends us to use those items. Especially as Jews, we have major problems in synthesizing the literal keeping of the commandment with the heart of the matter in some cases.

For example, the Bible instructs us to "keep the Shabbat day holy" and says that we should not do any menial labor or light fires on Shabbat. Today we live in a different world and so must ask ourselves what it means not to do any work or light fires in our modern context. When a person turns the ignition switch on in his car, is he lighting a fire? If a person turns on the electricity or opens his refrigerator, is he lighting a fire? Different Jewish groups have developed different answers to these questions, but they are matters that must be addressed when we try to keep Shabbat in an era of technology which the Bible did not ever mention. When we talk about *midrash* and *halacha*, we are addressing problems that have to do with life. This is not only theoretical theology because we actually create these kinds of *midrashim* all the time.

One example we have already discussed in a previous chapter was the problem of how congregations take tithes from their members. Texts are taken from the Tanach and the New Testament and are tied together to draw conclusions that are not explicit in either one of the original texts. This *midrash* is then applied to ordinary situations.

We must not allow ourselves to get frightened or withdraw when we hear the words "*midrash*," "Torah," "*halacha*," or "rabbis." There is no reason to be afraid of studying the Jewish background of the New Testament. It is a sin for us to try to make anyone Jewish. We should not tell anyone to keep Shabbat or to be circumcised or to keep any of these things unless he or she feels led by the Spirit of God to do so. Nevertheless, it is necessary to describe these issues because this is the world of the New Testament, and these are the kind of issues that the Apostles had to address. Additionally, these were the methods that were used in order to bring life to the early Church.

"*Halacha*" is simply a technical term which means the practical outworking of our daily life according to the Torah. How do we walk according to God's will? When one examines several of Paul's letters closely, it becomes apparent that they are divided in half. Normally, the first part is theological, and the next part is practical. The word that is the dividing line between the theological and practical part of the epistles is "walking." The first three chapters of Ephesians are very theological and theoretical, but then right before Paul begins giving a lot of specific, practical commands **Ephesians 4:1** says, *"...I urge you to **walk** in a manner worthy of the calling you have received."* The first part of **Colossians** is also very theological, but then **2:6** begins the practical section with the words, *"Therefore, as you received Messiah Yeshua as Lord, so **walk** in him."* *Halacha* is the way to walk practically as we live out our faith.

Paul was a Rabbi with a Rabbinic education, so he also wrote like a Rabbi. He studied with the best Rabbi in his generation. It should be no surprise then that he uses Rabbinic terms like "walking" as a way of life.

Another issue that has to be addressed when believers study the Bible's commandments is what Paul meant in Galatians when he spoke negatively about being "*under* the Torah." Since Paul says in **Romans 7:12** *"So the Torah is holy and the commandment is holy and righteous and good,"* he clearly does not mean that the Torah is a bad thing. Rather, the problem comes with being *under* the Torah. The key to understanding what being *under* the Torah means and why Paul saw it as negative is found in **Exodus 23:5**. This verse says, *"If you see the donkey of one who hates you lying down **under** its burden, you shall refrain from leaving him with it; you shall rescue it with him."* Here the Torah commands us to have mercy on this donkey that is so burdened by the load *under* which he is trying to walk that he cannot go any further. When we encounter this donkey, we are supposed to take his load off and free him so that he can walk.

Paul's understanding of the negative effects of being *under* the Torah comes from this passage. Therefore, to be *under* the Torah is to be so burdened by the Torah that one cannot live. It is possible to have such a legalistic spirit and approach to keeping the Torah, (which is not necessarily connected with the quantity of commandments one keeps, but rather to his attitude), that it does not allow him to freely walk. When a person is living *under* the load of the Torah, he is living *under* constant constraint and fear. One cannot function out of love and freedom when he is fearfully *under* the load of the Torah.

Does faith exempt us from keeping the commands of the Torah? There is a principle involved in this, and it relates to God's primary interests. Paul writes over and over again in his letters that Abraham was saved by faith, so this idea must have been an important underlying pillar to his worldview. **Romans 4-5**, **Galatians 3**, and many other places speak of the faith of Abraham and quote **Genesis 15:6**, which says, *"Abraham believed God, and he credited it to him as righteousness."* When Abraham believed, did he stop keeping the commandments of God? Abraham was saved by faith, but that faith brought him into obedience to the laws of God, just as **Genesis 26:5** says, *"Because Abraham obeyed my voice and kept my charge, my commandments, my statutes, and my laws."*

What then is Paul's point here? He is teaching that we become free from the *burden* of the Torah by the cross. The cross frees and delivers us from the *burden* of the Torah, not from the Torah itself. It frees us from the *curse* of the Torah. In **Galatians 3:13**, it says that through the cross we are free from the *curse* of the Torah. The Torah has entire chapters full of horrible curses, especially towards the end of Deuteronomy. What is the function of these curses? Their function purely and simply is *to instill fear!* These curses are designed to scare the people so that they would be obedient.

Europe has a lot of ancient medieval cathedrals with scary paintings of the Last Judgment on the walls. These paintings depict people being cut in pieces and beheaded and the devil swallowing them up. The purpose of these paintings is to instill fear, and the Torah has the curses for precisely the same reason. Nevertheless, wherever there is fear, there cannot be love, as **1 John 4:18** says, *"There is no fear in love, but perfect love casts out fear. For fear has to do with punishment, and whoever fears has not been perfected in love."* Whenever there is no love, the motivation for worshipping God is wrong.

God is not interested in sacrifices nearly as much as He cares about the love and motivations of our hearts. We know this from **Amos 6:6, Jeremiah 7:23, Isaiah 1**, and many other passages. God is not an idol who needs people to feed Him or build Him a house. He *needs* nothing from man. He *gives* everyone their life and breath and everything they have. What God is seeking from Israel and from the whole world is to have an honest and true relationship with Him based on the internal motivation of the heart of man. Love, freely given, is the opposite of fear. The reason we needed the New Covenant promised by Jeremiah was to free us from the fear and curse of the Torah so we are able to have a relationship with God and obey His *mitzvot* out of the love and honest motivations of our hearts. God was never interested in scaring the people into obedience. He always wanted a relationship based on true faith and love.

What changed when Yeshua died on the cross and was resurrected from the dead? **Galatians 3:13** says that when Yeshua died on the cross, He became a curse for us. Paul makes this *midrash* based on the same text in **Deuteronomy 21**, which we studied in the chapter on *kal va homer.* Paul uses the phrase *"cursed is the man who hangs on a tree"* from the Torah to explain why Yeshua was crucified. He became a curse for us. He did not die to take away the Torah but to take away the *curse* of the Torah. He died to free us from fear because fear was an instrument of the devil to enslave us. Yeshua freed us from the *burden* of the Torah because the *burden* of the Torah is not a positive thing.

The burden of the Torah was what Yeshua referred to when He condemned the Pharisees and lawyers in **Luke 11:46.** *"Woe to you lawyers also! For you load people with burdens hard to bear, and you yourselves will not even help the burden with your little fingers."* Yeshua's statements here refer to the matter of helping the donkey in Exodus, (which we have just addressed), as well as being a play on the words of King Rehoboam's advisors in **1 Kings 12:10-11.** They foolishly advised him to tell the Israelites who were complaining about the heavy taxes and forced labor that King Solomon had laid on them, *"My little finger is thicker than my father's thighs. And now, whereas my father laid on you a heavy yoke, I will add to your yoke…"* This is the problem with having a religion rather than a relationship with God. Yeshua came to free us from this problem, and He gave us His spirit to guide us into all truth. This is not so that we can do anything we want to do, but so that we are enabled to do the will of God. The easing of this burden is what Yeshua meant when He said in **Matthew 11:28-30**, *"Come unto me all you who are weary and heavily burdened, and I will give you rest. Take my yoke upon you and learn from me, for I am gentle and lowly in heart, and you will find rest for your souls. For my yoke is easy, and my burden is light."*

The reason we are supposed to "die with Yeshua" and be baptized is so that our own ego and passions no longer rule over us. They dictate to us, and without the help of God we stand helpless before them as **Romans 6** says. Now that we have been *"crucified with the Messiah,"* we have received a new life, an immortal life, in which we are guided by the Spirit of God and His Word and not by our own lusts.

In order to synthesize these two things, let as examine **Galatians 5:18,** which says, *"If you are led by the Spirit, you are not under the law."* Although it says we are not *under* the law, it does not mean that we are free to do whatever we want. Not being *under* the curse of the Torah means that we are no longer going to take part in the works of the flesh. Whenever there is an area of our lives that we have not yet submitted to the Spirit of God, the curse of the Torah still applies, however.

Let us clarify this matter. If we are obedient citizens and walk according to the laws of our country, we live in freedom. We are not afraid of the law. If we see a policeman, we can say hello to him or ask about his welfare or ask him for help. If, on the other hand, we have broken the law, and we see a policeman coming towards us, we immediately become afraid. We think, "Maybe he is coming to catch me. Maybe he knows what I have done wrong. Maybe my face will give me away." We then try to get away and not meet him face to face. On the other hand, if we are not guilty and have done nothing wrong, we have liberty! The law, in this case, has no effect.

Most of us still have areas of our lives which we have not yet submitted to the control of God's Spirit. We need the Torah to help us control the areas that have not been controlled from the inside. Paul's statement is conditional, *"If you walk by the Spirit, then you are no longer under Torah."* If we have not submitted a particular area to the Spirit, then the conclusion is that we are still in need of the Torah, and the Torah will be our judge. The Torah will be, in a sense, a fence to protect us from our own inclinations and weaknesses in these areas.

Moishe Rosen, the founder of Jews for Jesus, says that the problem with most believers is not that we do not have enough life; it is that we have not died enough in the Messiah. In our baptism, we did not really intend to give up our past.

We did not really want to give up all of our sins, and put them at the foot of the cross. We wrapped some of our old lives in a plastic bag, in a manner of speaking, and when we entered into baptism, that part remained dry. This is a problem in most of our lives. If we had died with the Messiah and were truly raised into a new life and were filled with the Spirit, the curse of the Torah would have no effect on us, because we would be doing the will of God. The Torah would be written on our hearts by the Holy Spirit, and we would automatically, from our internal motivations, be doing the will of God.

This is what Paul teaches. He was not teaching against the Torah. Anybody who teaches against the Torah is a false prophet. Paul could not teach against the Torah when he says in **Romans 7** that the Torah is from God and is a good and spiritual thing. In **Romans 3:31** he asks, "*Do we then make void the law through faith? Certainly not! On the contrary, we establish the law.*" In other words, we uphold and keep the Torah. What was crucified was not the Torah but the ***burden*** of the Torah. Paul could not say on one hand that the Torah is good, spiritual, and from God and then on the other hand say that the Torah is bad and dead.

Abraham was saved by faith, but he still had to obey the statutes, commandments, and precepts of the Lord. Whoever teaches that salvation by faith does not necessitate obedience is teaching against the will of God. Yeshua said in **John 14:15**, "*If you love me, you will keep My commandments.*" This combination of love and the keeping of commandments appears many times in the Tanach as well (c.f. **Exodus 20:6, Deut. 7:9, Dan. 9:4**). If we really believe that He is the Son of God, then we cannot deny that God's *mitzvot* and Yeshua's commandments are one and the same thing. We have been saved by faith so that we can be free to be obedient to God out of love and in purity of heart and mind and be servants of righteousness rather than servants of sin.

Chapter 6:

Messianic Jewish *Halacha*

The word "Halacha" comes from the Hebrew word "ללכת" - "to walk." It is a technical term used for the rules that govern life within the Jewish community. The term *Halacha* appears many times in the New Testament, especially in Paul's letters. Paul uses the word "walk" in some form in almost in every one of his letters when he gives practical instructions about the way the believer should conduct his life. Luke also uses this term when describing the way a righteous person lives. Here are a few examples of this point:

*"And they were both righteous before God, **walking** blamelessly in all the commandments and ordinances of the Lord."* **(Luke 1:6)[XVI]**

*"So that you may **walk** in a manner worthy of the God who calls you into His own kingdom and glory…"* **(1 Thess. 2:12)[XVII]**

*"Let us **walk** honestly, as in the day; not in rioting and drunkenness, not in sexual immorality and sensuality, not in strife and envying."* **(Romans 13:13)[XVIII]**

XVI   In this verse, "walking" is directly related to keeping the commandments of God.

XVII   This verse uses "walk" to refer to the righteous way of life the believer should follow.

XVIII   Paul's instruction to the Romans in relationship to the civil authorities is directly related to the keeping of the *halacha* that later the Rabbis formulated as "*dina demalchuta dina,*" (the law of the kingdom- Rome or any other pagan government- is the law).

*"But as God has distributed to every man, as the Lord has called every one, so let him **walk**. And so ordain I in all congregations."* (**1 Cor. 7:17**)[XIX]

There are many more examples of the use of this term "walk" in the context of *halacha*, but these are satisfactory to make the point. It seems clear from these passages that the First Century Church actively pursued the formation of a specialized Messianic *halacha*, and that it was referred to by the word "walk." There are also rulings and ordinances legislated for believers by the Apostles that do not specifically use the word "walk." Some identifying terms here would be "rule," "permit," or "prohibit." Each of these words has a corresponding Hebrew term that is widespread in Rabbinic literature. "Permit," for example, reflects the Hebrew *halachic* term מתיר that means "to release" or "give permission."

The Apostles understood from the words of Yeshua in **Matthew 16:19** that they had the right to "bind" and "loose" on earth. *"I will give you the keys of the kingdom of heaven. Whatever you bind on earth will be bound in heaven, and whatever you loose on earth will be loosed in heaven."* The words of Yeshua are clear if they are understood within the Jewish context of forming *halacha*. Yeshua gave the Apostles authority to make decisions that would be acceptable or "bound" in heaven as well as on earth.

This is the exact same authority that the Rabbis took upon themselves. *Midrash Tehillim* 4 says, "An earthly king makes a decree, and though his counselors request, they cannot cancel it. Whether they desire to or not, they obey his decree, but if the king himself requests, it is cancelled. But the Holy One

---

XIX   Paul here clearly is making a *halachic* ruling for all his congregations. He commands the people in the all the congregations to walk according to their "calling." If they are Jews (circumcised), they should not be walking as Gentiles (uncircumcised). This is a *halachic* ruling that he binds on all the congregations as an ordinance.

Blessed be He is not that way because whatever the Sanhedrin decrees, He obeys." Although the Rabbis seem to have taken their authority a little too far in this case, the principle is the same. Yeshua gave the Apostles the right to form *halacha* by His authority. These rulings must still be based on Scripture, however, and must not have the dictatorial *ex-cathedra* attitude that plagued the Church for so many years.

Before we discuss some problems and guidelines for forming *halacha* in modern Messianic Judaism, let us first closely examine the context of **Matthew 23:1-4** and what it implies for Messianic *halacha* today. The meaning of this passage for us today cannot be much different than the way the Apostles understood it in the First Century.

Yeshua and His disciples were a part of the world of the Pharisees in the Land of Israel during the First Century CE, and Yeshua had a Pharisaic world-view. Therefore, all the arguments He had with the Pharisees were "in-house" arguments between co-religionists. In the First Century BCE, the Pharisees brought a religious revolution to Judaism by saying that God's will can be known and discerned by any student from the Holy Scriptures. Before this great revolution and according to the Torah of Moses, the way to discern the "will of God" was to ask the Priest or the Prophet. When these two institutions were marred by corruption and Hellenism, the Pharisees developed a school of thinking that gleaned knowledge of "God's will" by studying the text of the Torah. Yeshua also thought this way, which is why the Gospels record so many arguments between Him and the Pharisees. Only because the Pharisees considered Yeshua to be "one of them" could they have come to Him with accusations and questions about washing hands and picking corn on the Sabbath. If He had been a Sadducee, they would not have even bothered to accuse Him. We all argue with the people who are closest to us and accuse those whom we know best.

Matthew 23:1-4 says, "*Then Yeshua said to the crowds and his disciples, 'The teachers of the Law and the Pharisees sit in Moses' seat. So you must obey them and do everything they tell you. But do not do what they do, for they do not practice what they teach. They tie up heavy loads and put them on men's shoulders, but they themselves are not willing to lift a finger to move them.'*" Why does the text mention that Yeshua spoke both to the crowds and His disciples? The point of mentioning the crowds as well is to show that these words are applicable both to the common people and to Yeshua's disciples.

If we want to understand these instructions correctly, we must first discuss the meaning of the term "to sit in the seat of Moses." Moses' seat has been found in a number of synagogues dating from the Mishnaic period. The Rabbi used to sit in Moses' seat, (which functioned as a pulpit), and give his *drasha,* "homily," after the reading of the Torah. Because of the revolutionary Pharisaic idea that studying and interpreting the Scriptures was the standard by which man could know the will of God, the Rabbis who expounded the Torah from "Moses' seat" had great authority and responsibility. These Rabbis, who were in the line of authority from Moses, had the right to exegete the text and draw practical or moral conclusions from it. This was the earliest method of forming *halacha* in the Jewish Community.

Yeshua declared that the teachers of the Torah and the Pharisees have the authority to interpret and create *halacha* when they are explaining the text of the Torah of Moses. Yeshua's words here do not give a *carte-blanche* to them to make *halacha* for His disciples, however. The statement limits them to the time that they "sit in Moses' seat," which means only when they are exegeting the text of the Torah in the synagogue.

We now need to clarify the words, *"you must obey them and do everything they tell you,"* because many things have changed in Judaism in the last two thousand years. In the time of Yeshua, the Rabbis had not yet given any official and authoritative teaching against Yeshua or belief in Him. Unfortunately, after two thousand years of "Christian" history, both the situations of the Jewish people and Christendom have changed significantly. During these years, Jewish tradition has made many polemical rulings against Christianity and Yeshua Himself. In my opinion, however, if we put the words of Yeshua back into their historical setting, we can obey them and still continue to respect the Jewish tradition of exegesis and interpretation of the Torah.

Yeshua's instructions to "do what the Pharisees say but not what they do" are interestingly similar to King Alexander Yannai's instructions to his wife, Queen Alexandra (Shlomzion) as recorded in bSotah 22b. He said, "Fear not the Pharisees and the non-Pharisees but guard yourself against the hypocrites because their deeds are the deeds of Zimri but they expect a reward like Phineas." It is apparent that Yeshua's problem with these Pharisees was that they made many rules from the Torah but did not keep them themselves. He opposed making demands and putting burdens on the people without consideration of whether it was practical or even possible to keep them. The Torah was given so that we could live by it. It is not meant to simply be a theoretical exercise for people living in a *Beit Midrash* who never have to deal with daily and practical problems.

The place to start creating *halacha* today has to be Yeshua's instructions to His disciples in this passage, so we are obligated to carefully consider His words. This passage implies that we must make a very serious effort to know, study, and understand what "the Pharisees who sit in Moses' seat" say and teach on a variety of issues that we all face as Jews living in a post-modern world. We must discover an operating system that allows us to respect and accept the traditional interpretation of Orthodox Judaism. At the same time, we must add elements of life, the guidance of the Holy Spirit, and a good measure of God's love and grace in the spirit of Yeshua's teaching. This may be the greatest challenge of the Messianic Jewish Movement today.

A follower of Yeshua must always take into account the principles of God's grace. Messianic Jewish *halacha* must stay as close to the Word of God as possible and remember that we will ultimately be judged on the basis of the grace of God through Yeshua's sacrifice. This grace of God, however, cannot be taken as an *a-priori* consideration for forming *halacha*. It can only come into consideration as a *post-priori* extenuation of circumstances. To explain this further, let us remember that laws are made on the basis of certain standards and not on the basis of exceptions and special cases. These exceptions are not supposed to be the norm. In the same way, God's grace should not justify making a more lenient ruling than the Torah demands in normal cases. If the normal standard cannot be met because of unavoidable and exceptional circumstances, then God's grace will cover that situation.

Let us now examine some potential problems with the forming of *halacha* in today's Messianic Jewish Movement. We need to be honest with ourselves about the fact that we lack much of the unity, equipment, training, and tradition to form our own body of *halacha* at this time. If we want to succeed, we have to work to increase our integrity in the eyes of the

Jewish and Christian communities. Since we lack important knowledge about the Torah and Judaism, our integrity as an authentic Jewish movement is in question in the eyes of both Jews and Christians. Additionally, as long as our movement depends on donations from Gentiles churches in order to exist, we will be subject to accusations of being potentially biased in our decisions.

Unfortunately, we do not have many leaders who are widely respected enough in the Messianic and Christian communities for their *halachic* decisions to be accepted by the majority of the Messianic community. When we do create a body of *halacha*, we have to make sure that we do so in a manner that is as detached from internal politics and power plays as possible. We also have to try not to be divisive by making "rules of conduct" that only a small minority will keep, while the others continue doing whatever they please. Sadly, most of the members of the Messianic movement hardly care about the *halacha* that is clearly written in the Scriptures, much less Judaism. If they do not even care about the explicit laws of God, they will certainly not care about what some leaders decide to bind on them.

Most importantly, we must not invent our own regulations if they take us out of fellowship with the rest of the people of Israel. There is nothing that will turn us into a sect faster than making our own *halacha* in opposition to Jewish tradition or in opposition to the New Testament's commands. We cannot start binding rules on our members that would widen the divide between us and the Jewish community. It may, in fact, be better, to simply accept the traditional *halacha* on every subject that does not directly impugn the person and character of Yeshua the Messiah or contradict the written Word of God. On the other hand, some congregations may find it preferable for demographic reasons to just settle for the Protestant model and follow the path of Christian White Anglo-Saxon culture.

These words may cut deeply and hurt, but without an honest assessment of who we are today, we will not be capable of forming a valid and credible body of *halacha.* Without this kind of painful honesty, any *halacha* we make will be short-lived and divisive to the Body of the Messiah and to Israel as a people. In short, if we are to create our own body of *halacha*, we need to do it very cautiously and with much prayer and consideration.

Rather than simply focusing on the potential pitfalls and problems inherent in constructing Messianic *halacha,* let us also review some important steps we need to take when we begin to navigate these challenging seas. The first guideline for Messianic *halacha* is that it must include acceptance of all the *halachic* rulings and Apostolic examples and inferences that we find in the New Testament. One of the basic rules for forming *halacha* is that one must build on the foundation of what the previous generations handed down as authoritative. We cannot create new *halacha* by ignoring or outsmarting the Apostolic writers of God's inspired Word. Ignoring the rulings of the Apostles will make the Messianic movement live up to the accusations of our Jewish brothers that we are a cult, and the Christian world will join the same refrain. Forming *halacha* cannot become a tool for resolving political problems in the Messianic movement. Rather, it must be a sincere search for doing God's will today in the Spirit and Truth of His Living Word. We must recommit ourselves to the fact that the Word of God alone is the authority for our teaching and actions.

The second step that we need to take as individuals and as a movement is to reason out our stance about the relationship between Biblical "commandments," God's grace, and our unity with the rest of the Body of Messiah. We do not want to alienate our non-Jewish, Christian brothers who are still stranded on the unbalanced shores of Martin Luther's understanding of God's grace. We want to present a reasoned out theology with a loving and friendly attitude without compromising the Word of God or the Jewishness of the New Testament. Please see the chapter in this book on the subject of commandments and grace for one possible synthesis of these important concepts.

Third, we must commit ourselves to unity and fellowship despite all the arguments and disagreements that might arise during the process of making a body of *halacha*. There are all kinds of potential disagreements, personality clashes, vested interests, and issues of temperament that can emerge during such strong discussions and deliberations. We must display a great deal of tolerance and civilized behavior toward one another, no matter how much we disagree. We must remember that the purpose of forming *halacha* is to work toward unity in both actions and doctrine. If our own *halacha* estranges us from each other or from the Jewish community, it would be better for us to discard the whole idea until we mature.

Forming Messianic Jewish *halacha* will take a great deal of time. It will take years to develop the kind of respect and prestige that is necessary for our community to abide by the rulings of a committee. If we are going to have Messianic Jewish *halacha* in the future, we will have to work hard to gain the respect and the authority of God and of the Movement. It will also take scholarship and education, and scholarship demands a long time to build and develop within a community.

It is my firm conviction that with much good will from the members of our Messianic community and a broad base of thoughtful and knowledgeable leaders, we can build a Biblical and Jewish *halacha* for future generations of Messianic Jews.

We must start by preparing sufficient moral and financial support for those who do the task and choose people according to their spiritual and intellectual qualifications as honest students of God's Word and Jewish tradition. Our *halacha* must be rooted in Scripture and the grace of Yeshua. One vital part of the development of Messianic Jewish *halacha* is for us to return to an authentic Jewish hermeneutic with the guidance of the Holy Spirit. In this way, we will be able to grow and develop into a healthy, strong, and unified Body of Messiah.

Chapter 7:

The Principles of Jewish Education

There are seven pillars of every Jewish community, which have allowed us to survive thousands of years despite incredibly difficult circumstances. In all likelihood, we would not have survived without these pillars. The first pillar is the synagogue and worship. The community must gather together and worship the Creator. The second one is the charitable duty of taking care of widows and orphans. The third pillar is called *Talmud Torah*, which means school for children. Without teaching the Word of God to children, there can be no continuity nor transference of values and culture. Therefore, this pillar is crucial. The fourth pillar is *Beit Midrash*, which means adult education. Jewish adults are commanded to continue to study the Torah throughout our entire lives. The Torah is eternal and is renewed by the Lord from day to day. Therefore, we see that education is very important to the Jewish community.

The other pillars include *mikveh* (ritual immersion), taking care of the poor, and caring for the dead, which means washing their bodies before burial, maintaining the cemetery, etc. In this study, however, we will concentrate on education and its importance in the Jewish community.

One of the greatest commandments in Judaism is to learn the Word of God. God saves the mentally disabled, the ignorant, and the mentally ill out of His pure mercy. Nevertheless, salvation is not the only thing that God wants from us. He wants us to be instruments and tools in His hand. God can turn a donkey into a prophet, and He even did this once in the case of Balaam and his donkey. None of us should strive to be a mere donkey, however. God can and does use people even if they are unlearned, but learning and studying the Word of God is essential.

Paul says to Timothy in **2 Timothy 2:15**, *"Study to show yourself approved to God, a worker who does not need to be ashamed, rightly dividing the word of truth."*

Showing ourselves approved means to justify the credit that God has given us. We have received credit from God by grace, but with the idea that we will grow in the faith and be useful to the Kingdom of God. If a person desires to be useful in any position or profession, as a housewife or mother, a carpenter, an electrician, or a doctor, then continuous growth is a requirement. Professional growth and growth in "professional faith" is vital because if given an opportunity to witness to someone about Yeshua, we must have the answers.

We are living in a world that is not as simple as it used to be a few hundred years ago because people have access to modern communication and a lot of information. Children at seven or eight years old already know how to surf the internet and search for things, and knowledge is power. Knowledge of God's Word is double power because it not only affects our lives here on earth, but also affects heaven. Ignorance has never been bliss, and education is one of the most important things in life. That is both the Biblical and the Jewish understanding of life. We are commanded to study and to show ourselves approved to justify the confidence and credit that God has given us. We are commanded to have answers from the Word of God and the Holy Spirit to give if somebody asks us to give a reason for the hope that is within us. Nevertheless, that is only one aspect of understanding and studying the Word of God.

Jewish people study the Bible universally by reading the same portion of the Torah in every synagogue all around the world on each particular week. No matter whether they are Reform, Conservative, Orthodox, Reconstructionist, or Messianic, all the Jews all around the world read the same text from the Bible every week. Once a year we publicly read and study through all five of the Books of Moses and parts of the Prophets in the *parasha,* (weekly portion).

There is a portion in Exodus which contains some very important things about education. Reading from **Exodus 12:25-27** we see, *"When you enter the land that the Lord will give you as he promised, observe this ceremony. And when your children ask you, 'What does this ceremony mean to you?' then tell them, 'It is the Passover sacrifice to the Lord, who passed over the houses of the Israelites in Egypt and spared our homes when he struck down the Egyptians.' Then the people bowed down and worshipped."*

When our children see us doing something, no matter what it is, they will ask, "What is this thing that you are doing?" As children grow up, they will ask questions like, "Dad and Mom, why are we going to congregation? Why do we believe in God? Who is this Yeshua? Why do you give money? Can't we stay at home? Can I stay home only this one time and watch an interesting show on television instead of going to congregation?" They will want to know what our lives are all about, and the answers we give our children will stay with them for the rest of their lives. They will not remain believers or walk in the light if we give them the wrong answers. They will know faster than anybody else if we are fakes, and they will know faster than anybody else if we have any equipment in our heads. Children know these things.

This section of the Torah is from the time that the people were still in Egypt, and it foresaw that after they entered the Land, the children would ask their parents, "What is this work that you are doing? What is your life about?" The answer that we give them has to be a proper answer.

Education is not only about how to make more money. It is a question of quality of life and how well we will perform our jobs and what equipment we will be able to use. A person can still turn some screws with an old kitchen knife if there is no screwdriver available, and most of us have done this once or twice. If one looks at the tip of the kitchen knife after it gets used in place of a screwdriver, however, it becomes clear that it is not ideal. We damage the knife, we damage the screw, and very likely, we could damage our hands because if it slips, it cuts us. It was not made for that. One cannot be a good musician without going to school, and one cannot even do a good job of cooking in the kitchen at home without learning how to do it. If we want to do something that is worth doing, we have to know how to do it correctly.

Apparently, the devil has deceived the Church and said, "You do not need to learn. Just sit on the Bible or sleep on the Bible, and somehow by osmosis, something will filter through to you." It does not work that way, however; study is essential.

In **Exodus 13:14-16** it says, *"In days to come, when your son asks you, 'What does this mean?' say to him, 'With a mighty hand the Lord brought us out of Egypt, out of the land of slavery. When Pharaoh stubbornly refused to let us go, the Lord killed every firstborn in Egypt, both man and animal. This is why I sacrifice to the Lord the first male offspring of every womb and redeem each of my firstborn sons.' And it will be a sign on your hand and a symbol on your forehead that the*

Lord brought us out of Egypt with his mighty hand."

One very important thing about the Jewish concept of education is that education involves signs. For example, in every doctor's office there is a diploma hanging on his wall that says from which school he got his degree, and it makes a difference which school he attended. No one wants a neurosurgeon that got his degree by correspondence. The diploma functions as a sign to prove that he received a genuine, high quality education.

God's education involves signs as well. God says that when our sons ask, "What are you doing here?" we must tell them, "God took us out of Egypt with signs and wonders and with a strong hand, and here is the sign that every Jew should have. He should have the word of the Lord between his eyes and on his arm as a symbol of his relationship with God and what God has done for him."

We all have symbols. Most people have wedding rings, and some churches have a cross. We also may have personal symbols that mean nothing to anyone but us. My wife keeps the pants that my son wore at his Bar Mitzvah in a trunk in the storeroom, even though they are so small now that we could not even make a sleeve out of them for his size. For her they have a special meaning.

Our schools and teachers are also symbols for our education, and they have value. I have had the good fortune of having some of the best teachers both in Judaism and Christianity. I was lucky to be born in the time slot in which some of the giants were still alive. I had the privilege of sitting under people like Martin Buber, one of the most famous Jewish philosophers. I have listened to them and drunk from the wells of knowledge that they had. I remember and still quote sermons that some of my teachers gave more than thirty years ago, not because I am so smart, but because I wanted to know what God had for me. I had to have the equipment to face my Jewish brothers and sisters and convince them, with the Holy Spirit's help, why Yeshua is the Messiah.

Maybe in America a person can say, "Follow me just because I am pretty and happy," but it does not work that way with Jews and Arabs or in most of the world. We must be able to give an answer for the hope that God has planted within us, and that answer has to come from the Word of God. We cannot give what we do not have. This is Principle Number One in education and in life. Now the question is where are we going to get what we want to give? We want to be God's servants so He can use us. He made us, gave us a nose, a mouth, a brain, and eyes, and God can use us if we want to be used by Him.

In order to be a priest in the Tanach, there were certain requirements. One had to be born into the family of Aaron, but even that was not enough. The men had to prepare from the time they were three months old until they were twenty years old. During all that time, there was no Temple service allowed. All this training was done in preparation to **eventually** serve. At twenty years old, they began to serve as apprentices to the priests until they were thirty, which is ten more years of preparation. They could only serve in the Temple from the time they were thirty to fifty years old. They prepared for thirty years because they could not make mistakes with the holy things of God. Making a mistake with the Temple implements could be deadly, as is clear from certain narratives in the Tanach.

Why did Eli's sons and Aaron's sons, the nephews of Moses, die? "Bringing strange fire" means that there was a correct place to get the fire for the altar, and they got lazy. They became lazy because they drank alcohol, and their inhibitions were lowered. They may have gotten drunk and said, "Why should we go over there to get the fire? There is fire closer to us over here." So they took fire that God had not prescribed and got killed instantly by the Lord. Priests, therefore, had to be very careful because they were dealing with God's holy things.

To be a pastor or a teacher of God's Word today is just as scary. **Yaakov 3:1** says, "*Let not many of you become teachers*" because it is a very dangerous job. The leaders of congregations are dealing with people's lives, souls, emotions, and family situations, and it is a tremendous obligation. I lose a lot of sleep about what I advise people in our congregation in Jerusalem because I see kids imitating me and saying, "When I grow up I want to be like Joseph or Marcia or one of the other teachers of God's Word." When I advise people whose lives or marriages are on the rocks, I have to be careful because what I say and put the Holy Spirit's approval on can either build their lives or destroy their lives. There is no job that is more important and has more responsibility attached to it than being a shepherd of God's flock.

There is no job that is more rewarding either, and I am not talking about financial rewards. I have great-grandchildren in the Lord spread all over the world, and there is nothing more rewarding than knowing that I have helped some of these people find Yeshua, be saved, and have their sins forgiven. There is nothing more rewarding than seeing them crucified and raised with Messiah to a new life. There are Jews and Arabs and Germans and Finns and Japanese and Brazilians, who were formerly pagans and who have come to the Lord through my help. There is a great reward for this and great happiness, but also a great responsibility. God expects me to share the truth and not just a bunch of nice words.

If we are called to be servants, ministers, pastors, teachers, or elders, it is very important to make sure we have the right equipment to do the work. It is impossible to teach what we do not already have and know. In order to have, we must receive. In order to receive, we have to sit down, do the work, and graduate.

One of the principles I mentioned is a sign, a sign of the education we have received from God. That could be a diploma or a life of service and the respect of the community that says, "This man knows what he is talking about when he speaks from God's word." The way God educates is interesting because He uses tests to see if people are faithful or not, even though this may be hard for us to accept.

One of the most famous tests in the Bible is the one that God gave Abraham. Abraham had waited years to have a son from his wife Sarah, and finally Isaac was born. Then when his son reached twenty years old, God came to him in **Genesis 22** and said, *"Take your son, your only son Isaac, whom you love, and go to the land of Moriah and offer him there as a burnt offering on one of the mountains of which I shall tell you."* We know God did this to test him because the previous verse says, *"God tested Abraham."*

What are these tests for, and did God really need to test Abraham? God could see into Abraham's heart to see if he was following Him and if he believed or not. The answer is that Abraham needed the tests! He needed the texts for the same reason every high school student needs tests. Most high school, elementary, and even college teachers are not so cruel and sadistic that they enjoy giving tests to students with the possibility that the students will fail. The tests are for the student to know where he stands so he can know what he has learned and what he has not learned. The test was made for

Abraham because God knew Abraham's heart, but Abraham needed to know how far he was willing to go to obey God. There is no Jewish education without tests.

Some places in America are trying to do away with tests, and this is a big mistake. God tests us, and without these tests, we ourselves do not know how far our faith will take us. Abraham's test became a symbol of great faith and dedication and willingness to sacrifice everything that is valuable for the sake of God and His Word. As a result of passing this test, Abraham became such a great symbol of faith that he became known as "the father of the faithful."

After Abraham's test, **Genesis 22:16-17** declares the reward. *"'I swear by myself,' declares the Lord, 'that because you have done this and not withheld your son, your only son, I will surely bless you and make your descendants as numerous as the stars in the sky and as the sand on the seashore. Your descendants will take possession of the cities of their enemies.'"* When he passed the test, there was a reward in which the Lord blessed him and multiplied him. Education, especially Biblical education, is essentially passing the test and getting the reward. Likewise, when someone trains dogs and horses, they give them a dog biscuit or a sugar cube when they do well.

That is also how God handles education. When God saw that Abraham passed the test, He rewarded him with His blessing. In every case recorded in the Bible where God tested people, they became a great blessing after they passed. Testing and rewarding are very important concepts in Jewish education. It is not enough to just sit on the bench and absorb and say, "Now I have learned how to do it." If we do not practice what we have learned, then we have learned nothing.

After I graduated from my Christian university in America, Marcia and I invited one of the professors over for dinner one evening. At that time he told me, "Joe, God is not going to be able to use you until you forget everything you have learned in this university." What I learned in the classroom was a bunch of useless knowledge in comparison to what I learned from my teachers outside of the classroom by observing how they lived, treated their families, prayed, and studied the Word of God on their own. What I saw in their lives was a life changing experience for me. Knowledge is important, but if it is not applied to life, one cannot serve God effectively.

The Rabbis have a book called *Pirke Avot,* "The Ethics of the Fathers," which says that if a person wants to learn for learning's sake, God will give him the opportunity to learn. If he wants to learn in order to teach others, God will give him the opportunity to learn for himself and to teach others. While those things are good, if a person wants to learn in order to practice what he learns, then God will give him the opportunity to learn, to teach others, to practice what he learns, and as a bonus, eternal life in heaven.

We do not study just for learning's sake. The Greek, pagan philosophers studied only for learning's sake, but Jews are more practical than that. We learn in order to put into practice and do something with what we are learning. When we put into practice what we learned, we are learning life. When we practice what we learn, we receive the opportunity to learn and to teach others and to practice that knowledge and eternal life in heaven as well.

Another statement in *Pirkei Avot* says that anyone whose practice is less than his learning will lose his learning. In other words, if we do not use what we have learned, we will lose it. On the other hand, anyone whose practice is greater than his learning will keep his learning and his practice and receive a reward in heaven. In Hebrew we say, "*Lo ha-midrash ha-ikar, elah ha-ma'asei.*" Learning is not the main thing, but doing is the main thing. We have to know how to do something before we can do it.

I have been using a computer since 1982, and I basically use a computer like a fancy typewriter because I do not know how to program it and have never programmed anything. I probably only use fifteen or twenty percent of the capabilities of my word processor, and it is capable of doing a lot more. It has been said that Einstein only used five percent of his abilities, and most of us probably do not even use that much! God can use any one of us to do mighty and wonderful things, but the secret is that we have to exercise our faculties and put them to work so that we can become useful to God and to His kingdom. None of us have reached even fifty percent of the abilities which God has given us. God's Word is a tool with which to exercise our minds.

People say, "Look at how successful the Jews are." There are more Jewish Nobel Prize winners than in any other ethnic group in the world. It is a fact that about fifty percent of Nobel Prize winners are Jews. Jews are neither born with higher IQs nor are naturally smarter than everybody else, but they have the stubbornness to sit down and do the work that it takes. We must have disciplined lives and a desire to please God and do the work. Without putting in the blood, sweat, and tears that it takes to learn, we cannot do the work. There is no magic to it; the only magic is sitting down in obedience to God and applying oneself to do the work. Statistically speaking, by the way, people who continue learning even until their old age are less likely to get Alzheimer's and lose their memory. The brain is like any other muscle; it has to be exercised.

One Biblical narrative that has great educational implications is about Elisha, the man of God, and comes from **2 Kings 4:8-36:**

"One day Elisha went to Shunem, and a well-to-do woman was there, who urged him to stay for a meal. So whenever he came by, he stopped there to eat. She said to her husband, 'I know that this man who often comes our way is a holy man of God. Let's make him a small room on the roof and put in it a bed and a table, a chair, and a lamp for him. Then he can stay there whenever he comes to us.'

"One day when Elisha came, he went up to his room and lay down there. He said to his servant Gehazi, 'Call the Shunamite.' So he called her, and she stood before him. Elisha said to him, 'Tell her, "You have gone through all this trouble for us. Now what can be done for you? Can we speak on your behalf to the king or the commander of the army?"'

"She replied, 'I have a home among my own people.'

"'What can be done for her?' Elisha asked.

"Gehazi said, 'Well, she has no son, and her husband is old.'

"Then Elisha said, 'Call her.' So he called her, and she stood before him in the doorway. 'About this time next year,' Elisha said, 'you will hold a son in your arms.'

"'No my lord,' she objected. 'Don't mislead your servant, O man of God.'

"But the woman became pregnant, and the next year about the same time she gave birth to a son, just as Elisha had told her.

"The child grew, and one day he went out to his father, who was with the reapers. 'My head, my head!' he said to his father.

"His father told a servant, 'Carry him to his mother.' After

the servant had lifted him up and carried him to his mother, the boy sat on her lap until noon, and then he died. She went up and laid him on the bed of the man of God, then shut the door and went out.

"She called her husband and said, 'Please send me one of the servants and a donkey so I can go to the man of God quickly and return.'

"'Why go to him today?' he asked. 'It is not the New Moon or the Sabbath.'

"'It is all right,' she said.

"She saddled the donkey and said to her servant, 'Lead on; don't slow down for me unless I tell you.' So she set out and came to the man of God at Mount Carmel.

"When he saw her in the distance, the man of God said to his servant Gehazi, 'Look! There is the Shunammite. Run to meet her and ask her, "Are you all right? Is your husband all right? Is your child all right?"'

"'Everything is all right,' she said.

"When she reached the man of God at the mountain, she took hold of his feet. Gehazi came over to push her away, but the man of God said, 'Leave her alone. She is in bitter distress, but the Lord has hidden it from me and has not told me why.'"

"'Did I ask you for a son, my lord?' she said. 'Didn't I tell you, "Don't raise my hopes"'?

"Elisha said to Gehazi, 'Tuck your cloak into your belt, take my staff in your hand, and run. If you meet anyone, do not greet him, and if anyone greets you, do not answer. Lay my staff on the boy's face.'"

"But the child's mother said, 'As surely as the Lord lives and as you live, I will not leave you.' So he got up and followed her.

"Gehazi went on ahead and laid the staff on the boy's face, but there was no sound or response. So Gehazi went back to meet Elisha and told him, 'The boy has not awakened.'

"When Elisha reached the house, there was the boy lying dead on his couch. He went in, shut the door on the two of them and prayed to the Lord. Then he got on the bed and lay upon the boy, mouth to mouth, eyes to eyes, hands to hands. As he stretched himself out upon him, the boy's body grew warm. Elisha turned away and walked back and forth in the room and then got on the bed and stretched out upon him once more. The boy sneezed seven times and opened his eyes.

"Elisha summoned Gehazi and said, 'Call the Shunammite.' And he did. When she came, he said, 'Take your son.' She came in, fell at his feet and bowed to the ground. Then she took her son and went out."

Elisha was a circuit preacher who traveled from place to place in the Jezreel Valley and Mount Carmel and did the work of a prophet. He prophesied and taught, and people came to ask him the will of God. Then a woman, who knew how close Elisha was to God and that he was a man of God, invited him over for dinner a few times. One day she turned to her husband and asked, "Why don't we make a small apartment for this man of God?"

There were no hotels in those days. People took the men of God into their houses, and they considered it a great honor. One important lesson within Jewish education is that a teacher must be valued. Teachers lived near their students and under their protection. Students supplied their teachers, just as the Shunammite wanted to supply a bed, a chair, a room, and a lamp- a place for Elisha to live. It is very important to Jews to value a teacher.

The New Testament commands in **1 Timothy 5:17** that the man of God who serves the congregation should be worthy of double honor. The words, "double honor" here mean "salary" or "money." He should be rewarded for his teaching if he is a man of God, but he should not have to ask for it.

This woman knew the importance of supplying a teacher, and so she wanted to build an apartment for the man of God. The man of God enjoyed living in this woman's house, and he appreciated it. So he asked her, "What can I do for you? Do you want me to talk to the king or the general on your behalf?"

She said, "No, I am living with my people. I am well connected within the community; I don't need your help."

Then the prophet's servant said, "This is what this woman needs. She has no child, even though she has been married many years, and her husband is already old. Let's pray for God to bless her." This is lesson number two in Jewish education: education is not one-sided. In the West, the teacher stands up on the platform, and the students sit down below him on the other side. The teacher gives, and the students receive.

In Judaism and in the Bible, education is a two-sided thing. The teacher gives and receives, and the students give and receive, just like the input and output wires in a stereo. In order to have real education, there must be input and output. Response is required in order to learn anything. It is important to argue, ask, and resist, or else there is no learning. The input and output can be of different substances, but if nothing is put in, nothing will be learned. If a person does not put something into his learning, either payment or homework or service work in the congregation or the community or taking care of poor widows and orphans or teaching little children, no education will take place.

The Greek model is that the teacher gives out, and everyone else receives. That is the Western, college model, but it does not work, which is why a lot of college graduates and even PhD's have very little practical knowledge. They are great in the classroom, but they, in effect, "do not have the sense to get out of the rain." The teachers from which I learned the most are the teachers whose relationship with me was one of input and output. When students give something back, both ends are happy. It is an important principle.

This woman had been good to Elisha, so he wanted to pay her back in some way. Therefore, he told her, "Next year at this time, you will have a son." God honored Elisha's words, and when the next year came around, she had a son.

When the son grew older, he went out to the field one day to work with his father and probably got sunstroke. His head started hurting, and then he died. The woman very dramatically rushed to the man of God who lived a couple hours away by donkey. Shunem is near Afula, and the man of God lived in the Carmel Mountains. It took a couple of hours to go get the man of God and a couple of hours to bring him back, while the child was lying dead on the couch. Then the man of God sent his servant and said, "Put my staff on the child's face," but nothing happened. When the man of God arrived, he put his eyes on the child's eyes, his head on his head, etc., basically something very similar to what his teacher Elijah had done when the son of the widow in Tyre died. Elijah took the boy to his room, lay on top of him, and prayed, "God, help this woman's child." God honored his words, and the child resurrected. This story with Elisha is very similar. He did what his own teacher had done. This is another important educational principle.

We are all like our teachers, and we all imitate them to some extent. Some of both my good and bad characteristics come from my teachers. I put a little of my own spice in it, but basically what I teach and know and the way I serve and function is what I learned from other people. God can use other human beings to fill us with His knowledge from the Word and from their experience. That is why not many of us should be teachers and why we should be careful about whom we allow to lay hands on us and from whom we are willing to absorb information. If I teach a bunch of garbage, then the minds and hearts of those who hear me will be full of garbage! If I teach what God's Word says, then those who hear me will have God's Word in their hearts. This is absolutely true, and it is inescapable. Teachers who are not equipped and who do not tell the truth will get their students in trouble. A good pastor does not allow people he does not know very well to teach his flock because if that "guest teacher" feeds the flock a bunch of garbage, they will get a stomach ache from it.

Elisha did what he learned from his teacher and rabbi Elijah. Since Elisha was Elijah's successor, he did what he learned from his teacher. We all do this, and it should be that way. By the way, one way to recognize that someone belongs to a cult is that they learn to imitate their teachers in an *exaggerated* manner. We have to be careful who our teachers are. We are all like our teachers, and as long as we do not become cultic and continue to remember who our ultimate guide and teacher is, we will be safe. We are all servants of God's in the long run.

Here Elisha came to the child in the room, and he became frustrated because the answer did not come from God immediately. He sent his servant to lay the staff on the child's face, but it did not work. When he came himself, it did not work at first either. We know this because the text says that he paced to and fro in the room, begging and crying out to God,

"This woman has blessed us, so we want you to bless her."

This returns to one of the educational principles mentioned before: one cannot learn without giving and receiving. If the pastor or elder or teacher only gives and does not receive, no education is taking place. Giving and receiving can be money, service, or many other things, but there has to be input and output on both ends. Otherwise people absorb and absorb without ever having learned anything. In the school of life, there has to be both giving and receiving. Here God honored Elisha, the child came back to life, and everybody went home happy.

One interesting question to consider is why this child died in the first place. God gave this child as an answer to prayer. The woman's husband was already old, and she had no son. Elisha told her by a word of prophecy, "Next year at this time, you will have a son." So why did this child die?

In a similar vein of thought, why did Lazarus, the friend of Yeshua, die? Yeshua stayed away for four days before He responded to Mary and Martha's call. They sent a message to Him in the Transjordan, and He could have arrived there in one day. He took His time, however, and did not hurry. He got there on the fourth day and had dinner. Everybody was crying because Lazarus had died, and only the next day when they went to the tomb early in the morning did Yeshua tell them to open the tomb and said to Lazarus, "Rise up." Then Lazarus came out of the grave, wrapped in his grave-clothes. Yeshua then said something very strange in this story: "He died for the glory of God."

This story with Elisha is strange in the same way because the woman was blessed, then her son died, and then Elisha resurrected him from the dead. What was it for? It was for their and our education. We learn nothing except through experience.

The faith of these people after they had experienced God was unshakeable.

I knew an Orthodox Jewish woman from the United States who became a believer and then immigrated to Israel. Since she was Orthodox, she began to study in a seminary for Orthodox Jewish women. When the rabbis found out that she was a believer in Yeshua, they decided to de-program her. Three rabbis sat with her and fired questions at her all night long and would not let her leave the room for any reason. They tried to brainwash her, and she sat there and listened to them. Finally the next morning, they all got tired and asked her what she thought then. At that point, they had laid in front of her all the objections they could think of about Yeshua, the New Testament, and Christianity. Nevertheless, she answered them with one sentence and completely devastated them when she said, "I'm sorry, but you cannot argue with an experience; I know Yeshua."

That is the essence of Biblical education. We are supposed to go from faith to knowledge. We are saved by faith, but God does not want us to stop with only faith. He wants us to **know** Him. God promised many times, "They will know me from the least to the greatest." He does not say, "They will believe in me" because belief is only the first stage. Paul says in **1 Corinthians 13**, the great love chapter, *"We will know like we are known."* He does not say "we will believe," but "we will know." There is no knowledge without education. It is wonderful that we believe in God and have innocent faith like little children, but we have to grow from faith into the knowledge of God. Without this testing, like Elisha and Lazarus, we will not get to knowledge because the difference between faith and knowledge is experiencing God.

I believe that a man landed on the moon, but I do not know it, because I was not there. I do not understand how he did it or how it works, but if I spent enough time studying physics and ballistics and all the different trajectories and how they landed, maybe I would know, rather than just believing. As children of God, we want to know and not just believe. Faith is a wonderful thing, but it is very fragile. When we know God and have experienced Him, we will be as strong as my friend and say, "You cannot argue with an experience. I have experienced God because I know His Word and put it to work. I see that it has power." That is what education is all about.

These are the simple basics of Jewish education: (1) There must be input and output. (2) We must value our teachers and choose whom we are willing to sit under. (3) We must be willing to suffer and sacrifice. (4) We have to experience and pass tests. (5) We have to put what we learn into practice. These are the essences of Biblical education, and there is no learning without these things. I have learned something from every person whom I have ever met, and this should be our attitude as well. Let us conclude with this expression: "I have gained wisdom from every one of my teachers."

Appendix:

The 13 Principles of Rabbi Ishmael[XX]

1. קל וחומר *kal va-homer* (light and heavy or *a fortiori*)

2. גזרה שוה *G'zerah Shavah* (equivocal expressions)

3. בנין אב מכתוב אחד *Binyan av mikatuv echad* (making up a "family" from one text) and בנין אב משני כתובים *Binyan av mish'nei ketuvim* (making up a "family" from two or more texts)

4. כלל ופרט *Kelal Uferat* (general to the particular)

5. פרט וכלל *Prat u'kelal* (particular to general)

6. כלל ופרט וכלל, אי אתה דן אלא כעין הפרט *Kelal uferat ukelal, i atah dan elah k'ein ha-perat* (general statement followed by a specification followed in turn by another general statement- one may only infer whatever is similar to the specification)

7. מכלל שהוא צריך לפרט ומפרט שהוא צריך לכלל *M'kelal sh'hu tzarik lifrat umiprat sh'hu tzarik likelal* (when a general statement requires a specification or a

XX   For a complete list of these principles in Hebrew and in English along with notes and examples for each one, please see any daily Hebrew-English Artscroll Siddur with notes. These principles are recited during *Shacharit* (the morning prayer service) between the recitation of the Torah passages about the daily sacrificial offerings and the *P'sukei d'Zimrah* (songs of praise).

specification requires a general statement to clarify its meaning)

8. כל דבר שהיה בכלל ויצא מן הכלל ללמד, לא ללמד על עצמו יצא, אלא ללמד על הכלל כלו יצא

Kol davar sh'haya bikelal v'yatza min hakelal lelamed, lo l'lamed al atzmo yatza, elah l'lamed al hakelal kulo yatza

(anything that was included in a general statement but was then singled out from the general statement in order to teach something was not singled out to teach only about itself, but to apply its teaching to the entire generality)

9. כל דבר שהיה בכלל ויצא לטעון טעון אחד שהוא כענינו, יצא להקל ולא להחמיר

Kol davar sh'haya bikelal v'yatza lit'on, to'an echad sh'hu k'inyano, yatza l'hakel v'lo lehachmir

(anything that was included in a general statement but was then singled out to discuss a provision similar to the general category has been singled out to be lenient rather than more severe)

10. כל דבר שהיה בכלל ויצא לטעון טען אחר שלא כענינו, יצא להקל ולהחמיר

Kol davar sh'haya bikelal v'yatza lit'on to'an sh'lo k'inyano yatza l'hakel ulehachmir

(anything that was included in a general statement but was then singled out to discuss a provision not similar to the general category has been singled out both to be more lenient and more severe)

11. ‏כל דבר שהיה בכלל ויצא לדון בדבר החדש, אי אתה יכול להחזירו לכללו,‏
‏עד שיחזירנו הכתוב לכללו בפרוש‏

Kol davar sh'haya bikelal v'yatza lidon b'davar hachadash, i atah yakol l'hachziro likelalo ad sh'yachzireynu hakatuv likelalo b'ferush

(anything that was included in a general statement but was then singled out to be treated as a new case cannot be returned to its general statement unless Scripture returns it explicitly to its general statement)

12. ‏דבר הלמד מעניינו, ודבר הלמד מסופו‏

Davar halamed me'inyano v'davar halamed misofo

(explanation obtained from context or from the following passage)

13. ‏וכן שני כתובים המכחישים זה את זה, עד שיבוא הכתוב השלישי‏
‏ויכריע ביניהם‏

Sh'nei ketuvim hamak-chishim zeh et zeh ad sh'yavo hakatuv hashlishi v'yakria beineihem

(two passages that contradict one another until a third passage comes to reconcile them)

Selected Bibliography

Allison, Dale C. *The Sermon on the Mount.*
New York: Crossroad Publishing Company, 1999.

The Babylonian Talmud: Glossary. Ed. I. Epstein. Index
Volume. London: Socino Press, 1952.

Ben Isaiah, Abraham and Benjamin Sharfman.
The Pentateuch with Rashi's Commentary:
A Linear Translation into English. Vol. 2. *Exodus.*
Brooklyn: S. S. & R. Publishing Company, 1949.

Fishbane, Michael. "*Midrash* and the Meaning of Scripture."
The Interpretation of the Bible: The International
Symposium in Slovenia. Ed. Joze Krasovec.
Sheffield: Sheffield Academic Press, 1998.

"Hermeneutics." *Oxford Dictionary of the Christian Church.*
Ed. F. L. Cross. Oxford University Press, 1983.

Keener, Craig S. *A Commentary on the Gospel of Matthew.*
Grand Rapids: Eerdman's, 1999.

Lategan, Bernard C. "Hermeneutics." *Anchor Bible*
Dictionary. Vol. 3. London: Doubleday, 1992.

The Minor Tractates of the Talmud. Ed. Rev. Dr. A. Cohen.
Socino Press,1971.

Neusner, Jacob. *Invitation to Midrash.*
London: Harper and Row Publishers, 1989.

Porton, Gary G. "*Midrash.*" *ABD.* Vol. 4.

Royerson, J. W. and Werner G. Jeanrod. "Interpretation, History of." *ABD*. Vol. 3.

Santala, Risto. *The Midrash of the Messiah.*
Finland: Tummavuoren Kirjapaino Oy, 2002.

Ibid. *Paul, the Man and the Teacher in the Light of Jewish Sources*. Jerusalem: Keren Meshichit, 1995.